Anatomy of the Future

RODERICK SEIDENBERG

Anatomy of the Future

Chapel Hill
THE UNIVERSITY OF NORTH CAROLINA PRESS

COPYRIGHT © 1961 BY

THE UNIVERSITY OF NORTH CAROLINA PRESS

MANUFACTURED IN THE UNITED STATES OF AMERICA

VAN REES PRESS • NEW YORK

Contents

		Page
Chapter 1.	Anatomy of the Future	1
2.	Dilemma of Form and Content	42
3.	Challenge of Intelligence	78
4.	Mirror of the Psyche	132

Note of Acknowledgment

To write about the future is to set oneself adrift in a sea of speculation. The writer must shoulder full responsibility for these hazardous explorations. They are, perforce, wholly personal. Nevertheless, my own venture was undertaken with many good wishes for a *bon voyage* from my friends, H. H. Wilson, Carl Zigrosser, Waldo Frank, Lewis Mumford, Leo Gershoy, Evan W. Thomas, and Hermann J. Muller. Their interest and encouragement sped me on my way.

I wish to express my appreciation, as well, to the John Simon Guggenheim Memorial Foundation for granting me a fellowship that enabled me to pursue this journey into the future.

R. S.

Doylestown, Pa.

Anatomy of the Future

CHAPTER 1

Anatomy of the Future

I

NEVER BEFORE, it is safe to say, has the world been so intensely aware of change. Our century has been an era of unparalleled movement and speed, of accelerated activity in all the turbulent and multitudinous aspects of life. Amidst this commotion we live in an atmosphere of expectancy, conscious of a future at once imminent and uncertain. Under the impact of our relentless momentum we seem for the first time in history closer to the future than the past, as though the very speed of our transit created a vacuum, a hiatus, between ourselves and our heritage. For more than three centuries now we have witnessed a rising series of innovations in virtually every aspect of life: in politics and economics, in commerce, agriculture, and industry, in science and technology, in art and architecture, in education and communication. And though the world has doubtless been subjected to greater changes during this period than any other in recorded history, we are avidly awaiting still greater, more far-reaching, more decisive changes. For change indeed is the dominant sign of the times, not only throughout Western civilization, but in the vast hinterlands of Asia and Africa as well. Today, strengthened by its own advances, this wave of change has reached the remotest regions of Kenya and inundated the once fabulous isolation of Tibet. The world is in transit; and men everywhere seem subject to a common tremor of anticipation, a universal sense of change.

What is the meaning of this universal tension? Are we on the threshold of some sweeping, as yet unplumbed transformation in the form and condition of human existence, a vast metamorphosis running the gamut of life? Or are we merely entering upon a further, if more spectacular, transition in the orbit of the past? Are we witnessing the birth of a new world, or are we merely continuing upon the path of a sustained development dating, let us say, from the time of the Renaissance? The question, clearly, is crucial in any attempt to assess the meaning and direction of our future course. But even more basic perhaps—as the philosophers of history will be quick to note—is the question of whether we may possibly confront the future, and in what manner we may do so, in the hope of discerning its lineaments. On what premises, whether of science or legerdemain, are we entitled to attempt the prognostication of the future?

There was a time, even as late as the Classical Ages, when men practiced divination by means of sacred auguries. Today this manner of prognostication is a lost art; and we are reduced to foretelling the future on the basis of some theory or conception of history, explicitly stated or implicitly assumed, as a continuous and meaningful process. Unfortunately, there is no consensus as to what that meaning is, or whether indeed history is a process having any meaning. Thus, at the very start of our inquiry, we find ourselves burdened with a formidable array of prior questions, the answers to which, in the nature of the case, may prove less than conclusive. But the enforced detour prompted

ANATOMY OF THE FUTURE 3

by these questions may nevertheless prove rewarding and perhaps even more illuminating than a direct assault upon the provocative problem of the future itself. Whatever the route, the compelling nature of the problem merits attention and invites speculation, for certainly the most challenging question confronting mankind today is the world of tomorrow.

II

It is not without significance that an increasing number of historians, whose province has always been the past, are concerning themselves with the future. However diverse their individual formulations and conclusions, they share a common if tacit belief that history is susceptible, in part or in whole, of some measure of extrapolation. That is to say, history is conceived in terms of a process, unilinear or cyclical, exhibiting a discernible pattern of trends or tendencies whose trajectory into the future is vouchsafed by their established and meaningful occurrence in the past. Predictability, however, is the hallmark of a science based on immutable laws. In claiming a like prerogative without a comparable scaffolding of historic laws and principles in the enigmatic field of human affairs, historians may well seem, in contrast to scientists, like vagabonds skating on thin ice. But if history has not yet attained the status of a science, historians may perhaps retort, with some show of plausibility, that the art which enables them to comprehend the past entitles them to speculate upon the future. Even in the cold and rigorous domain of science, intuition has been known to precede knowledge.

Admittedly, historians have thus far failed to establish any definable laws of historic development. Even the well-established nineteenth-century notions of progress and of a unilinear historic ascent have both been under heavy fire, if not discarded altogether. In one form or another these earlier conceptions of historic advance have been largely superseded by cyclical theories of cultures or civilizations. Apparently convinced of their errors in granting pre-eminence to their own culture under the illusion of an inherent principle of progress and a misconception of the laws of biologic evolution, historians now seem in danger of an opposite extreme. Having abandoned the progressive relationship of historic units, whether of societies or civilizations, as parochial, inept, and unwarranted, they are inclined to neglect the wider problem of any possible meaning in the historic process as a whole on the ingenious premise that there is no such thing. Oswald Spengler in particular subscribes to this astonishing view; and though Arnold Toynbee holds to a teleological interpretation of human affairs on purely intuitive grounds, he too is concerned chiefly with the rhythmical growth and decline of the specific civilizations he considers to have reached any degree of maturity. In his book, *Social Philosophies in an Age of Crisis,* Pitirim Sorokin, reviewing the works of Danilevsky, Spengler, Toynbee, Northrop, Schweitzer, Berdyaev, and others including himself, maintains with not a little asperity that the hitherto dominant linear conceptions of history are doomed to give way to rising philosophies of history of a cyclical, creatively recurrent, eschatological, or an Apocalyptic and Messianic type. With the possible exception of cyclical theories of culture, this assortment of historic interpretations seems to have little relation to any empirical, not to mention scientific, basis. The meaning of history is not to be found, apparently, within the confines of history as we have known it, but rather, according to this summation, in some far-off final judgment or in some equally remote, endless, purposeless, and perhaps indeed meaningless, repetition of cultural cycles. These various approaches do honor to the mystery of the problem and in an oblique, poetic sense, to a profound mystical hope at the heart of man, but the problem itself remains unresolved. The mundane story of the development of human history vanishes in the sunset flare of its transcendent ending.

Cyclical theories of culture, it will be granted, have an undeniable measure of validity. There is, for example, a definite parallelism between the disintegration of the Classical World and our own, as Toynbee maintains in his treatise on *The World and the West*. There are also, however, decisive divergences and unarguable differences that seem to outweigh any abstract comparisons on the basis of these disintegrating aspects. We need only to remind ourselves of our incomparably greater systems of communication and transportation, of our far-flung scientific technology, and finally of our enclosed world in which for the first time we are adjusting ourselves not merely to the surface diversities of nature, but far more significantly—due to our vastly enlarged scientific comprehension—to the underlying uniformities of the laws of nature, to perceive that the stage-setting is that of another play. In neglecting the space-time continuum of history as a whole, the cyclical theories of culture necessarily fail to take into account certain basic facts and phenomena of human development, such as the gradual increase and dissemination of knowledge, which have their own unique bearing upon the course of history and the evolution of mankind. As we shall have occasion to see, this factor alone, reacting upon the constant of human intelligence, has resulted in a kind of expanding trellis upon which in the course of time one civilization after another has come to bloom. Even the early civilizations of the Americas seem to have followed this course independently of the cultures of Asia and Europe. There are, in short, cumulative aspects of world history that demand recognition, and perhaps never more so than in our own age of impending unification in a single dominant world culture.

One difficulty confronting the historian in seeking to establish the principles and laws, or at least the direction, of history is the relative brevity of the process along with its amazing complexity. This combination of factors suggests in itself a fateful acceleration. The number of great cultural units comprising the story of human history to date, according to the historians mentioned by Sorokin, amounts to ten—and allowing for more restricted or local cultural developments, to no more than twenty-six! The point is noteworthy. Plainly, in respect to any attempt to establish scientific laws of history on the basis of a morphology of its dominant culture systems, these meager numbers are painfully inadequate and meaningless. The six thousand years of recorded history leave us, it would seem, with no clear-cut structural pattern of its constituent cultures and at best with only a general sense of the nature and direction of the process as a whole. Again, with respect to the time span of recorded history, it is instructive to bear in mind that a mere hundred generations, for example, take us back to the reign of Ikhnaton, Amenhotep IV, the Pharaoh of Egypt about 1375 B.C. whom J. H. Breasted characterized as "the first individual in history." A further two millenniums take us to the fringes of historic time. And though human behavior during the period of recorded history has responded to the challenge of life in a bewildering diversity of patterns, human nature, on the contrary, seems not to have changed perceptibly. Even in sheer mental capacity, anthropologists assure us, modern man does not differ materially from his remote progenitors. The fabulous tapestry of history is woven with the selfsame threads available to man from the beginning; only the pattern and design have changed. Yet, brief as the story of history may appear against the backdrop of man's entire development, it is possible to discern certain abiding aspects amidst the confusion of these changes. By and large, the pageant of history reveals, for example, an increase in the totality of human knowledge, an increase in the rate of social change, and an increase in the magnitude of social units. Moreover, if the more or less ephemeral systems of civilization comprising the tableau of human history are neither related in a direct linear progression nor repeat precisely some inherent cycle of rise and fall, it is none the less clear—looking at the imminent convergence of our contemporary world into a single, homogeneous, universal pattern of life—that certain basic strands are emerging from the profusion of past events into an ever more decisive and meaningful design. We are thus led to surmise that the crisis of civilization in our time has perhaps a universal meaning, not merely because, in contrast to the Classic World, it is indeed global in extent, but more significantly because it appears to be the harbinger of a single encompassing climax to the whole historic process.

By common consent, we live in an age of crisis. Today, social change throughout the world is subject to a universal acceleration. This unique situation, in itself but one of the many challenging aspects of the modern world, is hardly to be set aside as an accidental conjunction of events or explained away simply as a consequence of minor, fortuitous happenings in our immediate past. It is obviously true that large effects are sometimes occasioned by minor events; an avalanche may be caused by a rolling pebble, but only, it is to be observed, on a mountainside of sufficient and accommodating slope. Thus we are reduced to seeking the underlying trends and tendencies, and beneath these the antecedent conditions that will account for the situation we are considering. In the field of historic sequences this will often involve us in the forbidding task of pursuing a retreating series of causes, each one more inclusive than the preceding one. The problem, however, is not quite as bleak or impossible as it appears to be, for example, to Karl R. Popper who finds history devoid of meaning, or to Isaiah Berlin for whom it possesses neither trends nor tendencies, principles nor laws, on the basis of which the history of the future might be subject to prediction. On this accounting, we are simultaneously cut off not only from the future but in a sense from the past as well. Logic can go no further; and we are accordingly doomed to that piecemeal view of the historic process which keeps us safely within the bounds of the present advocated in turn by Friedrich Hayek. Behind the blank walls of this philosophy of history, logic-bound (to create an analogy with "muscle-bound"), lies the age-old dilemma of free will and determinism that haunts the historian in his search for immutable laws comparable to the unrestricted laws of the natural sciences.

Modern analysis has shown that most of the so-called laws of nature have a statistical basis. That is to say, the predictability inherent in these laws is of a macrocosmic rather than a microcosmic character. The validity of these laws thus bears a relationship to sheer numbers: the larger the number of individual components, the more certain prediction becomes; the smaller the number, the less certain. Astronomy, though it often deals with isolated phenomena, is no exception, since its laws are based upon those of physics, a field in which great advances have been made partly because the regularity expressed in the laws of nature is there insured by the extraordinary magnitude of the numbers involved in the domain of atomic structure. The validity of the laws of nature has thus been established without an infinite knowledge embracing each individual microcosmic element: in short, the miraculous edifice of science has been achieved without omniscience. In a similar manner the principles of hydrodynamics, for example, enable us to build adequate dams though they take no account of the foam and bubbles, the eddies and pools, accompanying the sportive descent of the brooks and streams that feed a given reservoir. It would seem sufficiently obvious that the historian, too, must accept the limitations of his finite mind in an infinitely complex world without flinching unduly. The macrocosm of history is not to be reduced to order by an infinite accretion of isolated facts, if such can be said to exist; nor is it to be abandoned, on the other hand, as an irreducible pandemonium of unrelated events. The dilemma of the historian, it is true, is aggravated by the very unpredictability inherent in the freedom of the individual human will. Actually, however, though the calculus of probability is restricted to mass phenomena, it is no less potent here than elsewhere. Long ago Immanuel Kant suggested that vital statistics concerning marriage in a free society had little relation to the whims of the individual—a point not without its wry humor in view of his own ambivalence in the matter. Finally, we dare not assume that our present limitations concerning historic predictability must necessarily be accepted as final. It is to be observed that atoms conformed to statistical laws before these were formulated; that the planets turned in their orbits and organic nature evolved before Copernicus and Darwin enlightened us concerning the principles involved in these manifestations of nature; and that history, likewise, may in time prove to have a structure of its own, though we await the coming of a Newton, as Henry Adams said, to reveal it to us. An a priori judgment questioning the very possibility of such ideas seems at least as unscientific in its assumptions as any of the tentative hypotheses concerning the meaning and drift of history as a whole to which Mr. Berlin and his school object so strenuously as being "conspicuously absurd." History, in all its vast diversity, may well seem a meaningless and unfathomable conglomeration of events, devoid of structure, of order, of human significance and direction; even so, its very chaos, unique in the panorama of nature, demands interpretation and challenges our understanding.

Actually, the dilemma of the historian in seeking to validate a measure of predictability despite the freedom of the will is not as final as the sheer logical statement of the problem would tend to make it appear. For without a sense of continuity the very idea of society vanishes into thin air, and freedom itself becomes meaningless. In the face of a future rendered unpredictable by the multitude of random choices open to the generality of mankind, individual freedom of choice must appear, to all intents and purposes, a futile and hollow gesture, if not an invitation to chaos. The notion of a structureless society, however, is an empty concept in which neither freedom nor predictability has a valid significance. Hence we may say there is a reciprocal, if inverse, relationship between freedom and predictability; to argue that individual freedom precludes the possibility of social prediction is not only to run counter to experience, but to carry the logic of the situation to a *reductio ad absurdum*. In the void created by this barren logic, all social planning, indeed all social enterprise, would be implicitly restricted to a mincing and inert sterility. On the basis of this reckoning it would be fatuous, moreover, to attempt to project or extrapolate into an unknown and unknowable future whatever trends or tendencies, whatever structure or pattern, the past may have exhibited, and historians in particular would be well advised to leave the future to future historians. But it is the nature of human consciousness, pragmatically as well as spiritually, to be uniquely aware of the future as an essential dimension of our "time-binding" endowment, in the apt phrase of Alfred Korzybski. For us, indeed, the future is incessantly and unavoidably present, consciously or unconsciously affording us a sense of potential continuity in which to meet the challenges of life. The depth and degree of our awareness of the future, reflecting our sense of the past, is a measure of our response to the ambiguities and uncertainties of our changing milieu; and thus, in turn, our sense of freedom is seen to be related to the stability or instability of the society to which we happen to belong. It is not without significance that the very idea of freedom, in the modern connotation of the term, simply did not exist in the primitive and fixed life of prehistoric society, if we may accept the word of anthropologists, and conceivably it may again lose whatever meaning it now has under the stability of a highly collectivized society in the future. The fact that for us the problem of freedom and predictability is seen in terms of a forbidding dilemma is but an index of our vertiginous rate of social change—a condition destined, sooner or later, to reach an implicit climax, after which the problem itself may well evaporate as the rate of social change, having reached its apogee, will once more decline and perhaps ultimately fade out in a static condition of permanence and fixity.

Meanwhile, in our day-to-day existence, we are confronted by real and momentous issues that serve to illumine the validity of historic processes and the momentum of historic forces. Though certainly no one, for example, favors world-wide nuclear annihilation, individual freedom to choose and act in the face of this supreme challenge has proved itself meaningless and bankrupt. Are we to conclude, in the interests of consistency, that the totality of individuals comprising mankind secretly prefers annihilation to the hazards of the future? Perhaps so. But surely it would seem more reasonable, by way of understanding this ominous stalemate, to grant a measure of reality to those trends and tendencies, those "vast impersonal forces" dominating our individual wills, which Mr. Berlin dismisses as the empty figments of distorted minds. The demographic situation threatening mankind, though less dramatic, is perhaps equally illuminating in revealing the impotence of the individual will in opposition to the spiraling drift of an overwhelming mass movement. Here the basic human instincts of sex and hunger, multiplied close to three billion times in their totality, have become, even in our day, an overriding world problem utterly beyond human solution on the basis of individual freedom of choice. Not logically, to be sure, but actually, pragmatically, historically. Again, in respect to the moral problems of war and peace, the position of the conscientious objector to war is essentially unassailable. But the tragic fact remains that his logic offers salvation only for himself; and though that logic is accessible to all, historic forces triumph over it in the recurrent passions of war. Plainly, however chastened we may be by Mr. Berlin's tirade against the questionable acceptance of the principles of historic determinism and historic inevitability, we must none the less acknowledge the sweep of underlying forces in their impact upon the structure of society and the direction of its development. For patently, these forces, arising out of the welter of human responses, take shape and become crystallized into tangible, often predictable, historic trends and movements. To deny the very existence of such historic forces is to separate the fabric of history into a meaningless series of isolated and unrelated facts; and to treat the course of history solely as the endless story of its individuals, past, present, and future, without regard to their complex interrelations, is to abandon all sense of social reality. It is the basic task of the historian to synthesize this vast material, to seek—however often he may have to revise or discard his hypotheses—precisely those significant forms and patterns of human behavior, those dominant, encompassing movements, that have given character and direction to entire epochs in the past, and beyond these, to the whole panorama of human history itself.

III

Had Julius Caesar fallen into the Rubicon instead of crossing it, the history of Rome might well have been different from what in fact it was; and had the youthful Hitler been admitted to the Vienna *Akademie* as an art student he might have indulged in execrable designs on paper instead of venting his spleen upon the world at large. At every turn history presents us with the opportunity of taking fanciful excursions into an unrealized future from the vantage point of some past event, some specific condition or situation. Such ventures, however, are rarely conceived in terms of a basic revision of man's essential nature, or alterations in his psychic structure, or changes in his dominant responses to the challenges of life. Samuel Butler essayed such an attempt, in a purely satiric vein, in describing for us the absorbing history of the Erewhonians, whose highly rationalized behavior led them, long ago, to banish machinery from their midst. The distortions and modifications history might have suffered as a consequence of fortuitous incidents in the past are seen to be wholly different in essence, scope, and impact from such more inclusive and permanent reconstructions of the past. They belong, we perceive, to a different order or category of historic situation. But this distinction in respect to the past has a significant bearing upon our attitude and approach to the future as well. Plainly, in our ignorance of its precise conformation, we cannot toy with the future as we may with the past; indeed, we shall have to reverse our approach and confine ourselves entirely to the probable trajectory of the more enduring, more basic aspects of human existence. In brief, we shall have to confine ourselves at best to its bare structural aspects, to what may be termed the anatomy of the future.

Prognostications based on this restricted manner of approach will necessarily remain abstract and generic, being concerned with factors of change in the basic structure and operative principles of human development; but that is not to say they will lack significance in bringing the future into focus. The sharpness of that focus, and indeed the validity of our prognostications, will come to depend not only upon ascertaining the nature and momentum of those basic historic forces that have molded our course, but upon determining as closely as possible their direction within the locus of our contemporary milieu. This aspect of the problem will entail an analysis of our highly complex culture in terms of its dominant forces.

It is clear, looking at the vast diversity and complexity of human history, that the life of man changes while the nature of man remains relatively stable. We have previously pointed to the arresting fact that during the span of recorded history—and indeed, according to anthropologists, throughout far longer periods of time—the innate capacities and endowments of the individual appear to have remained essentially unchanged. The history of man, however, is a panorama of change. How are we to account for this apparent anomaly? Plainly, the causes of historic change are not to be found directly in corresponding changes in the nature of man. They arise, we must assume, out of an abiding instability, a ferment, a profound dichotomy at the pivot of man's psychic constitution which caused him to deviate from the biologic hierarchy in the first place and, in turn, has sustained this deviation with increasing force ever since. This slowly accelerating, tangential departure of man along an orbit of his own was due, it is important to note, not to any decisive superiority in his instinctual equipment in comparison with other forms of organic life, but solely to his unique cerebral endowment and his unique faculty of speech. It is in the dynamic interplay of these component elements—of innate, unconscious instinct and deliberate conscious reason, supplementing and at the same time opposing one another in their cumulative impact upon the conditions of life—that we come upon the genesis and operating forces of human history. For man may be defined, in distinction to all other animate forms, "as an organism," in the words of Flinders Petrie, "that seeks always to undo its adjustment." Or, to phrase the matter in somewhat different terms, it has been maintained that man alone is a problem-*solving* animal. Actually, while all living forms that survive may be said to share this adaptability in some sense, man alone has the unique distinction of being a problem-*raising* creature. This faculty is at once the occasion of his travail and of his glory and the primary source of his great historic transformations.

While this definition is perhaps subject to exception in the case of those isolated, stationary cultures of "historyless peoples" that have occurred here and there in the past, it is essentially sustained in the history of mankind as a whole. Moreover, it is increasingly confirmed as the panorama of history unfolds itself, until in our day the business of *undoing* our adjustment has at length reached a sustained, deliberate, and conscious stage with the coming of the scientific revolution. Basically that revolution called forth an increasingly rational approach to our understanding of nature and at the same time an increasingly rational accommodation to our newly discovered knowledge and understanding. But this singular effort was not to be accomplished without a profound detachment from, and even disparagement of, earlier attitudes. Seen in this perspective, the origin and meaning of our present crisis must be sought not simply in the background of current events, but in the trajectory of human history as the pageant of a deep dichotomy within the human psyche. On this reckoning the roots of our present upheaval extend backwards into the farthest past—to that remote aboriginal time when man first became aware of a growing disparity between his pre-conscious impulses, drives, and desires and his conscious approaches to the challenges of life. And though, to be sure, every age is heir to the same prehistoric heritage, our age alone seems destined to witness a decisive climax in this long-enduring schism. That is the unique historic meaning of our era.

The conflicts and tensions between heart and head are older by far than their modern expression; indeed, they are older than history. Conceived in the more prosaic but also more comprehensive terms of instinct and intelligence, that struggle marks the entire course of our long development from the time when man first deviated from the biologic order to the present moment of inward strain and outward turmoil. According to Sigmund Freud, civilization has meant a widening of consciousness and an increasing repression of the instincts. Taking the whole of our development into consideration, we can readily perceive the cumulative aspects of this process. First and foremost, it is plain that the rate of change in the evolution of mankind has progressively accelerated. Second, in correlation with this situation, we must note the cumulative increase in human knowledge and the deepening of human consciousness. Finally, we must take account of the crucial fact that while the instincts are relatively fixed and stabilized genetically, the fruits of intelligence, being socially inheritable, follow a cumulative pattern. And in so far as these trends are rooted in the psychic structure of man, constituting indeed the mechanism of our involved development, we are justified in pursuing certain inherent aspects of their momentum along the curve established by their trajectory in the past.

In respect to the striking increase in the rate of change which has characterized our development from its earliest beginnings in the immeasurably slow advances of the Stone Ages, perhaps a hundred thousand, perhaps a quarter of a million, years ago, to the vertiginous rate of change to which we are now trying to accommodate ourselves, we may naturally ask whether we are in fact reaching a saturation point or climax with respect to change, beyond which we may experience a reversal or slowing down in this extended progression. In the present state of the social sciences, clearly, we do not know whether the sheer rate of social change has indeed a limit beyond which human society will be subject to a definite "change of phase," a climactic transformation in form and structure, as suggested by Henry Adams more than half a century ago. In our age of precipitate speed, progress, and change, we are impatient of limitations; yet modern man has in fact already reached certain inherent boundaries, certain *perimeters of the future*, which he can never surpass, and in respect to which progress must cease, if only because he has already attained an ultimate goal and final destination. For instance, the speed of communication, now, like the magic of *The Arabian Nights*, virtually instantaneous, cannot ever be surpassed.

In a somewhat similar sense we are led to ask: Are we approaching the threshold of a critical limit with respect to the ultimate rate of social change? For it will be granted that the functioning of any social system implies a measure of structured stability and continuity which must in time give way to chaos under the impact of ceaseless change. Before reaching such a limiting condition, however, society—if it is to survive—will have developed new modes and methods of procedure designed to insure that minimum of stability and permanence necessary for its purposes. But these conditions, as we shall see, are actually in process of being fulfilled beneath the rapidly changing aspects of contemporary life. To understand this complex situation more clearly, it will be necessary to explore the problem in all its aspects and, in particular, to clarify and establish the cause or causes, the origin and meaning, of the climactic crisis in which, by common consent, civilization now finds itself.

An analysis of current events, however illuminating in itself, will not suffice to bring the crisis of modern civilization into proper perspective. Nor have the bold attempts to establish a significant parallelism between the crucial upheavals and disintegrating phases of earlier culture systems and our own proved rewarding. Such attempts have failed not so much in what they have asserted as in what they have failed to assert. Committed primarily to a cyclical theory of civilization, the adherents of this philosophy of history are reluctant to grant that the present crisis has a world-wide significance, more sweeping, more decisive in character and more fateful in impact than previous crises. Their laboriously documented theories, based on a study of the past, appear strained when they attempt to account for the present situation as a mere repetition, in modern dress, of a drama common to all civilizations. For the unique feature of the impasse in which we find ourselves lies precisely in the fact that we are passing through a culminating movement of world-history itself.

Indeed, unlike the crises of earlier civilizations, our own is the first major phenomenon of world-history to be recognized as such—at least in the judgment of those not bound by a cyclical interpretation of all history. To be sure, the basic transformations that have marked the development of mankind—beginning with the introduction of fire, followed long after by the spread of agriculture, and later still by urbanization and the invention of writing—came in time to have a universal character, but they achieved this distinction only gradually in a world not yet aware of its global identity. The reverse is true of our own scientific revolution which, together with the prodigious technological innovations that accompanied it, constitutes a facet of prime importance in the crisis confronting us. It not only defined, it unified and consolidated and created, the world we know.

In certain respects the scientific revolution follows the pattern of earlier transformations in the history of mankind. In other respects it stands apart. Like the transformations of the past, it called forth an increase in population followed by more or less drastic changes in the form and structure of human society. These periodic increases in population, moreover, rose in an ascending curve, while the revolutions themselves followed one another in an ascending tempo. Thus far, as pointed out by Charles Galton Darwin in his provocative book, *The Next Million Years*, all the basic revolutions of man, being irreversible in character, have become universal in scope. In all these aspects the scientific revolution resembles the revolutions of the past.

It differs from these earlier revolutions, however, first and foremost in being concerned not so much with a specific change in the habits and customs of man as with a fundamental change in his manner of thinking—or, more accurately, with a fundamental change in the application of his rational faculties. One consequence, and possibly the most significant, of this essential difference is the fact that mankind therewith entered upon not merely an irreversible, but a sustained and continuous revolution whose trajectory into the future promises to augment our deviation from the past in ways beyond our reckoning. These unimaginable vistas, sustained by the spectacular achievements we have already garnered, serve to support our sense of a great watershed, as it were, in the development of mankind—a watershed dividing the past from the future by a decisive transformation in the structure, the meaning, and the direction of human existence. Thus, to mention but one phase of this vision, in finding ourselves the custodians of our own further evolution as well as that of the entire organic realm, as Julian Huxley has so ably demonstrated, we are entering upon an era of power, triumph, and responsibility altogether unique in the history of mankind. Beyond the ridge of the watershed we see a view of unexplored potentialities, and in the clearer atmosphere of our conscious awareness we perceive, in all directions, the challenge of a new world. But the vision of ourselves as conscious masters of our destiny is at once portentous and awe-inspiring, and nothing has given contemporary man greater pause than the ominous shadows he detects, even now, in this grandiose picture of the future. The suspicion grows that the source of these shadows lies behind him, in the world of the past—from which he imagined himself disengaged, only to discover that the mysterious lacunae of his new world are nothing but the forgotten realities of his former world. The crisis of our civilization lies hidden in the silent claim of these abandoned realities.

The earlier revolutions of mankind enriched the texture of life, slowly adding one aspect after another to the complex structure of civilization. Certainly the scientific revolution, more than any other, advanced this drift with startling rapidity. But in its sweeping and one-sided emphasis upon the rational component of the human psyche, it tended to denude if not denigrate earlier modes of apprehension. Thus the scientific revolution, oriented toward the past no less than the future in its all-embracing perspectives, has the unique distinction of adding a new dimension to the fullness of life while at the same time undermining and destroying long-nurtured elements of the previous orchestration of our responses. In doing so it brought into open and conscious conflict, for the first time in the course of our development, the profound schism that lay buried at the base of our psychic constitution. For we have reached, it is clear, a painful turning point, a moment of fateful instability, in the uneasy balance of our dichotomous natures. To comprehend the full depth of this impasse it is well to remind ourselves that behind the tense drama of modern life, with its manifold and complex involvements, lies a more encompassing drama spanning the whole of our evolutionary development. Like a spring tide, during which the sun and moon are in conjunction, the climactic nature of our crisis is due to a disturbance of universal scope, operative throughout history, augmented by the culminating impact of the scientific revolution.

For the moment it is this underlying conflict that engages our attention—a conflict between apparently incommensurable elements in the psychic structure of man. History, which has so often been interpreted in terms of conflict, whether military, economic, political, or spiritual, has rarely been viewed as the arena of profound psychic tensions. Yet our startling deviation from the biologic hierarchy in the dim recesses of prehistoric times, presaged in itself a drama of unceasing conflict. However unaware primitive man may have been of the nature of this divergence, he became in the course of time increasingly conscious of an isolating principle, so to speak, that set him ever further apart from the womb of nature. Along with its moral purport, the myth of the Garden of Eden, like many similar legends, presents the role of knowledge as mysterious, awesome, and sacred. For it was knowledge, in its deep social bearing and cumulative aspects, that served as a moving fulcrum for the lever of man's intelligence in causing him to deviate ever further from his earliest instinctual responses to the challenges of life. And though, from the beginning, man sought to achieve a harmonious synthesis through all the varied phases of his cultural development, in which the stability of his instinctual responses would be merged with the dynamic impact of his rational procedures, he has never found an enduring and satisfying solution to this dilemma at the core of his being. On the contrary, with the passage of time the rift has widened, while the effort to heal it has resulted in an acceleration of change, until in our day this chasm runs, dark and forbidding, into the landscape of the future. For we have come at length to a decisive imbalance in the relative influences of instinct and intelligence in the conduct of life, an imbalance, moreover, that was implicit in the dichotomous structure of man's psyche from the beginning. The moving factor in this equation of primary forces is clearly the cumulative nature of human knowledge, and on the basis of this factor alone it is evident that mankind was destined sooner or later to reach a wavering equilibrium between them, after which their roles would be reversed and intelligence rather than instinct would exert the dominant influence in structuring the ever more complex responses to the challenges of life. The varying phases of this vast and inherent transformation in which man sought above all to translate the nameless realm of his unconscious being into the explicit forms and patterns of conscious thought were at last concentrated, clarified, and brought to fruition by the scientific revolution. And in consonance with this goal, man sought to embrace every phase and aspect of life, for the first time in history, under a rational panoply.

Summarizing what has been said, it is clear the crisis in our civilization is unique in being the scene of a fateful reversal in the relative influences of instinct and intelligence—a reversal implicit in the historic process owing to the dichotomous structure of the human psyche. But this profound reversal, actualized in a continuous series of changes following upon the advent of the scientific revolution, implies a sweeping reorientation of man's procedures, a turning point and change of direction in his affairs different from any previous transformation in his experience. Thus the crisis in our civilization is seen to be more than a contemporary impasse; it constitutes, instead, a culminating phase of the historic process as a whole.

IV

It is time, however, to bring this crisis into sharper focus, to examine its present meaning and more immediate context. Thus only may we hope to add a final setting to the direction of the trajectory implicit in the trends and tendencies of the past. Having established the fact of their momentum, we must now enter upon a more precise determination of their direction.

Instinct and intelligence are terms equally difficult to define. Like many basic terms, they are at once too narrow and specific to carry the wide range of ideas attached to them, or again too vague, shopworn, and imprecise to satisfy their rigorous use and application. Unfortunately, the art of definition consists largely in shuffling words about from one statement to another without end—a process that frequently leads to the coining of entirely new and often uncouth expressions of Greek or Latin extraction which serve like a house without an address for disposing of the problem. It is not without significance that instinct is a term shunned by modern writers though it has a precise meaning in biology and an assured niche in psychology, as witness the works of Freud, for instance. On the other hand, intelligence, though equally impervious to exact definition, enjoys the widest possible currency; it sustains our faith and hope in science and technology, in politics and economics, in education and social organization,

ANATOMY OF THE FUTURE

and not least of all in the future of mankind itself. Nor is it without significance that neither art nor religion is represented in this random tableau of activities, for their roots find nourishment in another domain and at another level of our psychic constitution. The blunt rejection of one term and the ready but largely uncritical acceptance of the other reflect the temper of the times and reveal in themselves a crucial change of emphasis in our psychic orientation.

When mentioned in conjunction with one another, instinct and intelligence convey a sense of polarities, the one conscious, the other unconscious in its essential orientation. This distinction can be amplified into a wide range of attributes, conscious and unconscious, embracing on the one side the rational, analytical, deliberate and purposive aspects of the mind—faculties capable of highly abstract and generalized relationships—and on the other the less precise intuitive and emotional sensibilities of the mind, which, involved more with ends than means, endow life with its manifold values. Between these disparate aspects a complex web of relationships exists, a kind of antiphony that has often marked successive epochs in the past history of man. Thus the Middle Ages of faith were followed by the temporal, outwardly oriented Renaissance; the Enlightenment, with its emphasis upon empiricism, by a later reassertion of naïve feeling in the Romantic movement of the poets. Even today, the methodical rationalism to which we seem wholly dedicated has called forth a dark and countervailing irrationalism. In part, these reversions, or perhaps it is better to say antiphonal responses, seek to effect a cultural synthesis of the divers aspects of the human psyche—a harmonious orchestration of man's complex being. In part, they represent the swing of the pendulum between the polarities of his being as action and reaction assert themselves in a struggle for dominance. But if the pendulum in our era seems rather to have swung permanently to one side, assuring the dominance of the rational over the instinctual propensities of the psyche in a decisive sense, we must interpret the meaning of our age not as a temporary foray, a provisional triumph, but as a true and irreversible transformation—a final metamorphosis indeed, embracing the whole of existence.

In contradistinction to such an eventuality, it has been the belief of humanists throughout the past, substantiated by the great cultural achievements of mankind, that an enduring amalgam of man's dichotomous nature was in fact an attainable ideal towards which humanity must strive in each age with renewed courage and faith. Goethe is the outstanding apostle of this philosophy in modern times. In our own day this faith has received expression in a bold and imaginative appeal by Julian Huxley who, speaking as a scientist, voiced the need of a newly conceived humanist religion appropriate to our age and time. The need underscores the absence of that unitary response Huxley advocates if we are not to fall victims to disintegration and collapse. The theme of a unitary philosophy has drawn support from many converging lines of modern critical thought; the same basic concept, however differently expressed, is to be found in the works of such men as L. L. Whyte, Erich Fromm, F. S. C. Northrop, Erich Kahler, and above all Lewis Mumford and Waldo Frank, to mention but a few among many. But a grave question now arises: Can our age, committed to an overwhelming technological establishment, dominated by a pragmatic rationalism that is sustained, in turn, by our phenomenal scientific achievements, and dedicated wholly to the means of life (glorified by a vast organizational revolution into a life of means)—can a civilization thus oriented achieve an antiphonal answer to itself? The challenge is clear and ominous. The final answer lies with the future, to be sure; conceivably, however, it will be given, not in the language of the question, but on the basis of values alien to our own and in terms fashioned under a wholly different orientation of human affairs.

Meanwhile, we are increasingly perturbed, increasingly suspicious, that a provisional decision in the direction of our course has already been reached with little or no hope of an imminent reversal.

Our very concern with the future reveals a heightened awareness, a sense of expectancy beyond the customary demands of life. Clearly, we are approaching the end of an era. And despite the pleas of philosophers and poets, humanists and visionaries, despite the voice of irrationalism or the acute anguish of modern art or the pious intonations of religious sects, it is apparent the swing of the pendulum is destined to continue its tangential course, away from rather than towards the compensating values and ideals of the past, into new and uncharted regions. We have broken with the more optimistic seductions and sustaining faiths of the past century to find ourselves in an altogether harder, more engrossed, more desperate world, in which the moral restraints and compassions, the accepted codes and conventions of an earlier day have lost their timbre. The attitudes and values upon which they were based have become obsolete, along with the humanist tradition out of which they arose and to which in turn they contributed. Even the doctrine of human progress, nurtured since the time of Francis Bacon and brought to bloom in the nineteenth century, has been rudely challenged, if not deflated. In all the dominant aspects of our milieu we seem to be diverging ever further from the complex counterpoint of inward value and outward achievement that has characterized Western civilization since the Renaissance. Instead, we are committed to an ever more searching manipulation of the raw world of external fact and concrete reality. And though this pursuit, carried forward with extraordinary finesse and subtlety, has led us from a knowledge of atoms and cells to that of the most distant nebulae, it has also left us exposed to fateful contradictions and dilemmas in the everyday pursuits of life. If we have made unprecedented scientific and technological advances, we have witnessed at the same time appalling moral regressions and incredible spiritual disasters. Plainly, we are moving in contrary directions; and perhaps the most arresting aspect of the situation lies in the suspicion that our dark regressions are in fact the obverse side of our spectacular advances—that somehow they are latent in the dissociated state of our civilization.

In response to the steadily increasing pressure of our technological development during the past hundred years or more, we now find ourselves at an unsuspected impasse in which the means rather than the ends of life are in our command. For the more intangible aims and goals of man have become dissipated and obscured beneath the staggering proliferation and perfection of his mundane means. In this eclipse the expanded world of modern technology has usurped the status of an autonomous realm with its own procedural techniques and its own modes and principles of social integration and social utility. Once severed, the ends and more particularly the means of life exert a polarity of their own as it were, a tacit or explicit influence reflecting the limitations of their own spheres, upon the structure of society and the nature of its values. In this dilemma we are desperately attempting to function according to the dictates and demands of one world while rendering capricious obeisance to the moribund ideals of another. But this situation, in the nature of the case, cannot long remain static, and our imbalance, growing ever more onerous and pronounced, must sooner or later reach a fateful turning point in the guiding attitudes and values of life.

It would be helpful to believe that we are confronted by an essential choice rather than an irreversible drift in the tableau of contemporary events. Perhaps, indeed, no single factor of our complex civilization appears in itself overwhelming and decisive. Even those aspects of the modern world which lend support to the idea of a critical climax in our historic development may well seem—judged by their own light—merely isolated and incidental phenomena rising out of the profuse heritage of the past. Viewed separately, they resemble islands on the horizon whose underwater topography remains to be discovered. Yet, taken one with another, their combined presence at this juncture of events constitutes an indefeasible challenge. We are witnessing the concerted emergence of new procedures and responses, of new techniques and attitudes, called forth by unique and unprecedented conditions in the affairs of mankind. For the moment we can at best only surmise what the probable effects of the sudden and extraordinary expansion in the means of life, or the continuous impact of our machine technology and the triumphant sway of science, or the vertiginous acceleration in the rate of social change and the startling accumulation of knowledge, or finally, to pile one extreme upon another, the sheer and incredible increase in world population along with the equally striking increase in organizational procedures in every phase of modern life, may be upon the form and structure of human existence in the future. We may be certain only of the fact that these vast and irrepressible trends, cemented by a common urgency, constitute in their massive interrelations a close-knit and sweeping determinism, a converging world movement.

This world movement—however it may be defined—is taking shape in its dominant aspects under the panoply of rationalism: the opposition to that movement, in so far as our more or less unconscious rejection of its aims are cogent, articulate, and recognizable, is based upon intuitive and emotional affirmations. At the same time, it is to be observed, this vague and ill-defined disparity, functioning under the intricate conditions of our technological milieu, has resulted in a growing divorcement between our mundane means and our more ultimate ends. Moreover, the structure and purposes of our dominant activities are everywhere calculated to enhance the welfare of the community rather than that of the individual. But this is merely to say the means of life in our increasingly complex civilization are socially determined, while the ends of life, becoming ever more diffused and ambiguous, remain the province, no less than the burden, of the individual. Thus the tension exerted by these forces grows progressively unequal, and the widening antinomy between the form and content of our civilization threatens to become final and complete. Under these circumstances the recoil into irrationalism in modern life has taken many forms, all of them tinged by a measure of protest: in politics it has given us an oblique escape into fascism; in philosophy it has given rise to existentialism and the desperate pursuit of Zen Buddhism; in aesthetics it has given rise to modern art. It is perhaps this later response which merits closest attention, if only because it emphasizes, by its very extremity, an essential aspect of our contemporary dilemma.

The basic dissonances of modern life, born of a crisis between conscious and unconscious loyalties and procedures, have nowhere been reflected with more searching eloquence and freedom than in the world of contemporary art. Beginning as a tumultuous movement of protest against "the faithful reproduction of the familiar," in the phrase of André Breton, modern art rapidly split into a number of schools seeking a new approach not alone in respect to content, but to the manner of vision and presentation, to the attitude and orientation of the artist himself. But in freeing himself from the trammels of accepted aesthetic conventions, the modern artist has flown to the four corners of his own psychic world. And in doing so he has given expression, often enough in wholly unconscious ways, to a profound alienation. Art is the sensitive reflection of the movements of life; indeed, it often presages these movements. Today it is deeply concerned in one way or another with the repercussions of the conflict between rational and irrational, conscious and unconscious motives, compulsions, and influences in their decisive struggle of attrition. The modern artist has been moved to explore the primal sources of creativity in his own newly penetrated "mental landscape," the irrational world of the unconscious where the causal laws of the external world are in abeyance, and where, as in the world of dreams, there are no logical contradictions to the free flow of his imagery. These excursions into the unconscious depths of feeling and symbol have found their widest expression in the visual arts, in sculpture and painting, perhaps because vision, preceding the spoken word, affords the closest intimacy with the basic sources of human emotion. However baffling and incomprehensible, there is, plainly, more than a nihilistic meaning in the challenging ambiguities of modern art; rather it is as though the creative impulse of the artist, rising against the impact of our ascendant rationalism, had been shattered and fragmented—witness, by way of example, those canvases of spattered forms, like exploded wallpaper, or those calmly ironic withdrawals into the domain of the irrational in the aloof visions of the surrealists, or those equally remote explorations of geometric forms and spacial abstractions that seek surcease in sheer mechanical joy. The first represent an act of dissociation and even of revolt; the others of escape, triumphant in their isolation from the bondage of a rationalized and confined world of conscious meaning. If the art of today has found refuge in a world of dissociated feelings, in a kind of alienated narcissism, it is because the cold wind of rationalism has dried up the inner sources of that organic vision which, flourishing in all high periods of art, sustained the mood and power of the grand styles of the past. Today that wind has scattered the spores of creativity in all directions, and the contemporary artists have, in the words of Malraux, "broken with the world," each after his own fashion. For they have no choice but to see themselves as essentially extruded individuals, isolated at the periphery of things. Thus uprooted, the intuitive, non-rational sources of their art find expression in an egregious display of aesthetic experimentation and bravura, of individual mannerisms and isolated, often esoteric and incomprehensible gestures.

Sir Herbert Read has summed up their plight in the following trenchant words: "The source of power in the artist is given by society, and that is precisely what is lacking in the modern artist. —'Uns trägt kein Volk.' We have no sense of community, of a people for whom and with whom we work. That is the tragedy of the modern artist, and only those who are blind to their own social disunity and spiritual separateness blame the modern artist for his obscurity."

Perhaps the art which comes closest, not to a compromise, but to an integral acceptance of rationalization, is architecture. Nor could it well be otherwise, for it is the function of architecture to express the temper of the times, to accept its technological demands, its rationalized procedures, and its organized "modular co-ordination." Nor is it surprising to discover that modern architecture displays, for the first time in history, a common idiom and a universal style, visible from Tokyo to Chicago, from Helsinki to Buenos Aires. Nevertheless, even in this field a protest has been voiced against the extreme puritanical functionalism promulgated, for instance, in Le Corbusier's famous definition of a house as a machine for living. This revolt was merely an effort to reaffirm the human balance, so irrelevant in a purely mechanical solution, between what might loosely be termed the introversive and extroversive aspects and functions of a building. Thus the blank walls of the contemporary dwelling are often adorned, as if by an instinct for counterpoint, with an example of contorted sculpture, an exotic plant or African mask, or perhaps a fragment of bleached driftwood that recalls by its very absence the now extinct life-force. Strands of emotional, instinctual impulses in the human psyche, banished from the design of the house, reappear in decorative antithesis. Even the fireplace—an anachronism in this age of thermostatic heating systems—is brazenly retained in de-

ANATOMY OF THE FUTURE

fiance of engineering logic to recall the magic of another world.

It is not without significance that modern art has consistently been frowned upon by dictatorships, whether to the right or the left. For modern art is predominantly a gesture of revolt in which the world is seen awry, and the distortions of the human face and figure serve to reflect in adult grimaces the frustrated human psyche. Beneath the bureaucratic opposition to modern art we cannot fail to perceive a profound conflict between the overriding principle of mass conformity and compliance under the totalitarian authority of the state, and the spiritual principle of the freedom of the individual. The Nazi regime had a sinister term for this process—*Gleichschaltung*—the arbitrary conformation of the masses under the total mobilization of the state. Whatever aspect of the human spirit could not be subdued and brought to its knees, as it were, was summarily rejected as an antisocial deviation. Nor is this situation confined solely to dictatorial regimes: under the subtler forms of "togetherness" and a thousand other social compulsions, we exercise a similar constraint upon the freedom of the individual. Thus the artist and poet, alienated under the persistent affirmation of pragmatic values and consciously oriented objectives, are merely prophets crying in the wilderness of a rationalized world. The revolt in the world of art turns out to be largely a revolt in the name of art against a mechanized, collectivized world of blank conformity.

Before leaving this aspect of the subject it may not be amiss to append a personal experience bearing on the psychic contrast between modern and traditional forms of architecture. While awaiting a bus on a corner of Madison Avenue in New York during a snow storm, I noticed the peculiar fact that not a flake of snow settled on the sheer glass sides of the huge, modern office buildings that lined the streets. Not until, looking southward, the eye rested on the apse of St. Patrick's Cathedral was one aware, suddenly, of snow delicately fringing each buttress, each corbel, each bit of tracery, with a lace-like, magic touch. The contrast was extreme and revealed in a moment the alienation of modern man from nature, his supreme indifference to its moods, his almost truculent disregard of its ever changing aspects. We live, plainly, in another world—a world of harsh unconcern, of flat contempt, if not defiance, of anything unrelated to our immediate purposes, our consecrated efficiency, our bland devotion to the practical demands of the system of things. In these vast and uncompromising structures, behind their sterile, utilitarian façades, we live truncated lives, unaware of the subtler aspects, the meaningful testimony of a larger, more mysterious world. And by a curious irony, "Madison Avenue" has come to be a term of facile subterfuge, of an elaborate and counterfeit grimace upon the face of America.

V

It may be well to consider now, in our study of the vast underlying forces that appear on the horizon of the future, the relationship between the individual and society. For the individual, as the agent of consciousness and the source of all potential creativity, is the ultimate vehicle of our knowledge and understanding, our values and spiritual enlightenment. We are thus led to ask: Are the form and structure of our increasingly collectivized society geared to enhance these potentialities? Or, contrariwise, are they destined, silently and unobserved, to eventuate in a transmutation of values under which the individual as such will be driven ever further into a peripheral position until at length he is absorbed and lost in the final anonymity of the average—a number among mere numbers?

If the artist in our society seems poised in a void, seeking an acceptable niche in the scheme of things, the individual per se has patently lost ground as a significant entity in the social body. There are a number of reasons in explanation of this deterioration in his status. Broadly stated, all the previously mentioned factors bearing upon the question of a crucial transformation of human society—the expansion in the means of life, the impact of our machine technology, the increase in human knowledge, the acceleration in the sheer rate of social change, the vast increase in world population and the natural enlargement of its social units, the emergence of organizational procedures in every aspect of life, and the dominance of rational, scientific methods of operation—all these factors contribute in establishing the fabric of a new social structure in which the role of the individual must necessarily become secondary to that of the community as a whole.

Now, it may be objected that the individual as such did not exist in primitive society and that history accordingly might be interpreted as a process of emancipation in which the person, in his potentialities as a conscious being, achieved at length the high attributes of spiritual and intellectual freedom. But the present erosion of the status of the individual, his descent from a heritage of infinite worth as his birthright to a position of an anonymous cog in the machinery of the state, runs fatally counter to this spiritual affirmation. At first glance we seem to be in the presence of a startling reversion, rendered all the more surprising in view of the fact that history presumably follows an irreversible path. Actually, of course, the situations are only superficially comparable. For the nature of primitive society, from which the individual could in no valid sense liberate himself, was utterly different from the consciously structured society of today in which the individual is held fixed by the arbitrary mandates of its collective power. Quite apart from the crucial difference in sheer magnitude, primitive society resembled in many respects an *organism*, while modern society, translating implicit constraints into explicit restrictions and compulsions, exhibits, on the contrary, the nature and attributes of an *organization*. But in this distinction we come upon a profound cleavage in the nature of human relationships. For the modern individual, unlike his archaic ancestor, is subject at the same time to a drastic extrusion, a deep alienation and atomization, counterbalanced by equally drastic centripetal forces that serve to hold him in a rigid orbit of social compulsions. Isolated, he is yet held firmly within the gravitational field of society by the force of its collective pressure. The cohesion of primitive society was based upon an unconscious acceptance of traditional habits, customs, and taboos; that of modern society is based upon an explicit series of rules, regulations, and laws deliberately framed to achieve the harmonious integration of the community on the basis of more or less axiomatic social principles. Thus, along with the distinction between a social organism and a social organization, we come upon an equally decisive and parallel difference between preconscious and conscious principles of social co-ordination. In the light of this perspective, the now vanishing freedom of the individual is seen to have been an ephemeral ideality that marked an era of final conflict between an earlier and a later mode of social integration. As that conflict approaches its end, the freedom of the individual will likewise disappear under increasingly standardized forms and patterns of behavior established on the basis of statistical averages and the greatest good of the greatest number. In so far as the individual differs from this average, he runs counter to the texture of society; and the burden of this difference increases as the mesh of social relationships becomes inevitably more explicit and decisive. Thus we have at least prima facie evidence for believing that the culture of the future, like that of the remote past—though for quite contrary reasons—will disavow the cult of individualism as an antisocial disease.

And though this shift in the status of the individual is a consequence of our more conscious approach to the challenges of life, it is in no sense to be interpreted as a deliberate objective of this change in approach and attitude. On the contrary, it is an inherent by-product of the extraordinary expansion of organized modes of operation in every aspect of modern life. This striking phenomenon, considered in and by itself, has received virtually no critical attention. Yet, under the compelling necessities of modern existence, organization is at once inherent and inevitable, a basic means on which the functioning of all the other means for the orderly and systematic operation of our complex and intricate civilization depends. In lieu of the cultural bonds of earlier societies, organization constitutes the structural scaffolding of our society. Nevertheless, though we brush shoulders with the obvious fact of organization in virtually every facet of modern life, we have remained singularly unperturbed by its ultimate implications, its morphological meaning, and its inherent impact upon our changing milieu. Plainly, the philosophy of organization remains to be explored. Accepted as the necessary *modus operandi* of our system of things, the sudden acceleration of organized procedures throughout the world, with all its far-reaching effects upon the form and texture of modern life, has aroused no uneasy concern, no speculative curiosity, about the consequences and goal of the trend. We are convinced apparently, in the depths of our practical wisdom, that where there is no alternative, there is also no problem. But the challenge of organization lies precisely in its inherent necessity and its inevitable expansion. We are thus led to ask: To what degree of organization are we committed? To what end will this vast and basic shift in the structure of society and the fabric of human relationships carry us? We are moving obscurely in a field of unprecedented forces. Viewed in the light of history, it is apparent that we have in fact come upon an abrupt change of direction in our traditional procedures, if not indeed—in the language of Henry Adams—upon a basic "change of phase" in the structure of human society.

Postponing for the moment, at this juncture of the argument, any questions concerning the ultimate meaning of organization or the significance of its universality or the range of its implications, it may be pertinent to ask on what basis we may anticipate the continued expansion of this principle into the foreseeable future. Theoretically, of course, as we shall have occasion to note, organization demands further organization, as order demands increasing order, in the efficient operation of any grouping—a principle that implies, in itself, an ultimate condition of universality. On a more concrete basis, however, there are a number of reasons sustaining this abstract conclusion. Our highly geared, immensely complex machine technology, with its intensification of speed in all the means of life, constitutes one reason; our vastly accelerated population growth constitutes another. There are of course many other factors sustaining this trend: the husbanding of natural resources, the expansion of scientific knowledge, the speed and universality of modern communication. Apart from the direct impact of our machine technology, the so-called population explosion may well prove to be the most salient factor in the organizational drift of the future. For the increase in world population, on the scale now threatening us, involves demographic problems of totally unprecedented sweep and urgency, far beyond anything the sheer increase in the magnitude of social units alone would imply.

The phenomenal increase in world population growth, confined almost entirely to the last two or three centuries, is sufficient in itself to indicate our entry into a transformed world. To appreciate the force of this point it may be well to mention the diagrammatic illustration of population growth from the beginning of recorded history to the present in Harrison Brown's admirable book, *The Challenge of Man's Future*. Nothing could be more revealing or dramatic than the right-angle turn which the growth line takes in passing from a virtually horizontal representation of population growth up to about the middle of the seventeenth century to the almost vertical ascent representing

ANATOMY OF THE FUTURE

growth in the modern era. At the present moment the population of the world is approximately three billion. This figure is augmented, each day, by an estimated 180,000 new births. By way of contrast, the estimated population of the world throughout prehistoric times is thought to have remained relatively stationary at about ten million—the present population of New York and its environs! This staggering increment is due almost entirely to the fivefold increase in world population that occurred during the last few centuries. It is anticipated, moreover, that the present total population figure, increasing at an alarming rate, will be doubled within our century, reaching six billion!

Mere numbers are apt to numb rather than kindle the imagination; in order to appreciate the decisive character of our demographic challenge we must bear in mind that we are now rapidly approaching a stark impasse in respect to the three primary factors of food supply, natural resources, and population growth. Not until these three variables are brought into a harmonious balance that ensures adequate standards of living can we hope to escape the overshadowing fatality of the problem. But such a solution, it is clear, will demand a degree of world organization beyond anything we have experienced in the past. The point merits elucidation, for it is not only the massive complexity of the problem in all its endless ramifications, but the inherent nature of any possible solution to this challenge, that marks our entry into a new and different world.

Even in the present state of our international relationships, population pressures are no longer localized in their effects, and nothing short of an eventual world solution can possibly assuage the incalculable miseries following upon overpopulation in any of its parts. But such a solution, as we have noted, can only be effective through the instrumentality of human intelligence functioning within a global framework. Yet the problem itself, it is well to note, arises in the first place out of the natural, unmodified expression of individual human desires: the primary, instinctual needs of hunger and sex. Thus, viewed in its widest aspects, the problem serves to focus our attention upon a drastic antinomy within the human psyche itself. For the elementary act of instinctual response, implicit in the biological primacy of survival, now presents itself, multiplied virtually three billion times, as a collective problem—a problem which instinct, left to itself, cannot envisage and which intelligence alone can possibly resolve. In the conscious recognition of this dilemma, involving a basic opposition between instinct and intelligence, we enter upon an essentially new era in our approach to the challenges of life.

The three factors of food supply, natural resources, and population growth each demand a high degree of organizational control in any solution involving an adequate measure of predictability. Both the food supply and our natural resources are in a measure dependent upon available energy, and it has been assumed that in time nuclear energy will materially hasten the solution of this aspect of the problem. It is apparent that nuclear energy itself, however, will demand a very high degree of organization if it is to become effectively available in amounts commensurate with the scope of the problem. Finally, the solution of the more basic population question will likewise demand an unprecedented measure of social control and social organization. All too clearly, moral exhortations in favor of continence are unlikely to resolve a problem rooted in the basic instincts of man. Mahatma Gandhi sought to relieve the grave threat of overpopulation in India by preaching a philosophy of moral restraint; his followers, significantly enough, have deemed it necessary to institute a deliberate, government-sponsored policy of artifical birth control. If the stark and tragic consequences of overpopulation are to be averted, or even ameliorated, the problem will have to be approached on a world-wide basis in respect to both population control and the conservation of natural resources. But such an

ANATOMY OF THE FUTURE

approach will be effective and meaningful only in the degree to which human society will have become collectivized within a framework of universal organization. Thus a problem arising out of the primary instincts of man will either have to be abandoned to the cruel checks and balances of nature or resolved under the deliberate and conscious direction of human intelligence. If the problem is new, the solution of the problem will demand a degree of social mastery and social organization that are equally new.

The drift towards increased organization in the modern world is due, however, to a number of factors, all of which, like the threat of overpopulation, are certain to become more, rather than less, compelling in the future. The factor of predictability in the functioning of our intricate machine technology alone demands an ever increasing measure of organized co-operation and co-ordination. Moreover, to attain maximum efficiency the equations upon which predictability rests must embrace the human element no less than the technical and the mechanical; and the detailed organization of society both as producers and consumers becomes correspondingly mandatory. For a profound symbiosis holds man and machine in a mutual relationship. Nor is the vaunted freedom of automation likely to relax the tension of this relationship. Under the stringently co-ordinated system of our machine technology, even the increase in leisure hours has somehow left us without a sense of leisure time; and the hapless individual, trying to make the most of his psychological Sabbath, finds himself adrift in a vacuum of meaningless isolation. (When the five-day work week was instituted by Macy's department store, it was discovered that not a few of the employees wandered about the premises on their extra day off to avoid the trying boredom of their newly won isolation!) Plainly, as the lattice of organized society spreads outward in patterns of ever more inclusive scope, the individual is left with less meaningful leisure, less chance and opportunity for the expression of his personal waywardness or idiosyncrasy—in brief for the spontaneity of creative impulses and the free play of the human spirit. For the nonrational components of the human psyche which nourished these impulses under a less regimented scheme of things will have become dispersed, their influence shattered, their contribution to the balance of society disrupted, while the seared residue of feeling and intuitive perception that is left will have been diluted and corrupted through the prevailing influence of our mass media.

Modern man is passing through a profound revolution in turning from preconscious to conscious modes of social procedure and social cohesion. In the course of this long-drawn-out transformation, society will be relatively vulnerable, under the conditions of constant change, to chaos and collapse. The vast increase in the sheer means of life, the unprecedented expansion of human knowledge, the ever increasing rate of social change, all combine to expose modern society to rapidly shifting conditions, to instability, and to confusion. Under these circumstances the drift toward organized modes of operation and procedure becomes increasingly necessary and inevitable. But the drift itself is not the product of a conscious decision; on the contrary, it arises out of the implicit necessities of the situation, out of the constantly greater need for integration and co-ordination in the functioning of our highly complex civilization. Nor is this drift confined to totalitarian regimes, however much they may invite it. A significant parallelism envelops the world in respect to the basic need of organization, and despite the eruption of contrary movements and irrational upheavals, it is clear the dominant sway of organizational procedures must in time encompass every phase and aspect of life. Inherently organization moves towards universality. In view of this principle, it would appear that mankind is destined to follow an apparently irreversible course leading to the eventual collectivization of human society and the atomization of the individual in a vast organizational transmutation of life. Indications of this drift are even now everywhere at hand, and though the principle of organization is concerned solely with the form and structure of society and its activities, it constitutes, by the force of its inevitable expansion, a basic key to the future condition of man.

It is apparent that the emphasis upon a universal and basic structural change in the nature of human society is in harmony neither with any of the cyclical nor with the now discarded linear interpretations of the historic process. Rooted in what is conceived to be a fundamental antithesis between instinct and intelligence, the entire span of history may be regarded as a transitional era in a profound metamorphosis during which mankind has been subject to the deep travail of changing from the once dominant influence of the instincts to that of our rational proclivities. Under the triumphant sway of science and the universal impact of our machine technology, we are approaching, it would seem, a climactic turning point in this metamorphosis. Our own convulsive era, taken in a wide sense, is thus seen to have a unique historic significance, and our grave concern with the future is but the intuitive apprehension of our entry into a new world, different from any known in the past.

CHAPTER 2

Dilemma of Form and Content

I

AERONAUTIC ENGINEERS, having devised missiles that far exceed the limit of speed human beings can tolerate, are now experimenting with ways and means of improving human endurance under extreme flight conditions. A somewhat similar problem may be said to confront the social scientists: How can man adjust himself to the vastly increased acceleration of his own civilization?

The spectacle of man vainly trying to catch up with himself is not without an aura of irony, but the more one delves into the challenge of this modern quandary, the more ominous it appears. Changes in the affairs of mankind seem suddenly to have spread and quickened like chain reactions of ever greater scope and momentum. Plainly, a vast upheaval is in the making, as change now follows upon change with alarming rapidity and mounting confusion. From about the middle of the eighteenth century onward, when man first became aware of this expanding process of change, he was, at least in the Western world, inclined to hail the phenomenon under the name of "progress" as a kind of beneficent social escalator. Whether he moved forward in response to his own will or not, society as a whole seemed to advance automatically into ever new regions of change, expansion, and improvement, and in the first flush of enthusiasm it was thought but a matter of time until humanity would surely reach the Heavenly City of the Philosophers. If the course of history has somehow failed to take us there, it is certainly not for lack of progress—at least in some directions. But all too obviously an undertow in the complex play of forces veered mankind from this shining hope. The astounding advances of man since the eighteenth century were confined, it is apparent, to augmenting his powers over nature, rather than to clarifying his sense of direction or enriching his values. In giving wings to his material achievements without a corresponding enlargement of his moral vision and spiritual insight, modern man, despite his high hopes and increased powers, now finds himself more desperate and harassed than ever.

As the modern world spun through accelerated cycles of change, of innovation, development, and invention, the previously accepted forms of social cohesion, rooted in established customs and traditions, proved ever more inadequate. The world of new devices, of new conceptions and operations, demanded an appropriate framework of procedures in the form and structure of society geared to its more complex relationships and vastly enlarged enterprises. Thus the world changed—socially, politically, and economically. But more profoundly the attitude of man changed, especially after the doctrine of evolution became more generally acknowledged, through a basic acceptance of the idea of change itself. The picture of a static world gave place to that of a dynamic world; movement, expansion, and aggression seized the imagination and served as steppingstones to a new interpretation of man's relation to nature and to himself. Looking back upon the Industrial Revolution, for example, we can see with W. H. Sheldon that it was in large measure an extroversive movement; and, in a like sense, the extension of the world to the limits of "The Great Frontier" (in the meaningful phrase of W. P. Webb) constituted a vast extroversive movement of expansion, potent even today in the grandiose visions of future interplanetary voyages. This new, externally oriented world of power, energy, and enterprise, of material exploration and exploitation, encompassed within a locus of secular ends and aims, of specific goals and defined purposes, called forth an increasingly concrete and explicit system of social control and social cohesion. In consequence, the tried balance between conscious and unconscious factors in the formation of social procedures suffered a progressive disruption in favor of deliberate control and administration, of planned management and direction. Now, especially, do we face an insistent demand for further organization and increased co-ordination in every phase and aspect of contemporary life. Beneath the turmoil of modern existence, beneath the very tension of international rivalries, the world moves steadily towards more deliberately formulated and orderly patterns of procedure. But these procedures are not evolved imperceptibly in the course of time like sacrosanct rituals of primitive society; they are intentionally contrived and consciously integrated in their specific roles as functional elements in the fabric of society. And however diverse their functions, whether economic, industrial, political, or social, these procedures are certain to be co-ordinated in a systematic and above all premeditated manner with the prevailing aims and ideals of existing society. For we live in a world that is moving, irreversibly it would seem, towards a condition of total organization.

This encompassing drift towards organized procedures thus spreads throughout wider areas of social life in an increasing tempo in response to perpetually recurring social demands. But the drift, it is worth noting, expands not so much in the manner of an organic growth as of a method of interlocking extension in

DILEMMA OF FORM AND CONTENT

which one unit after another falls into place, not unlike a jigsaw puzzle, in an over-all system of external relationships. Meanwhile, the pressure of the system increases in proportion to its extension, until finally the system as a whole exercises a necessary and irreversible domination. Eventually, the smallest interstices of the social fabric become involved and are drawn into the general scheme of things. Thus we have learned to accept, without any sense of incongruity, such moral anomalies as organized charity and such ironic antipodes as organized leisure and organized recreation. Everywhere the conscious, deliberate, purposive aspects of life overtake us, transforming existence into an elaborate pattern of serried means and planned procedures. Even education and religion, conceived as means rather than as ends, have long since become aggressively institutionalized, while the function of government has grown prodigiously since the time when Thomas Jefferson could say, without fear of uttering blasphemy, "That State governs best which governs least." Today, indeed, at least half the world has accepted the diametrically opposite concept of the totalitarian state—a vast superstructure of absolute authority functioning through a monolithic system of increasingly organized relationships. But this trend, as noted earlier, is not confined to totalitarian dictatorships, however much it may invite acceptance by them. The same drift is apparent within the looser framework of democratically constituted countries, in which the lag of tradition still operates and in which, in any case, the direct will of an oligarchy is either absent or disguised behind the façade of representative government. However covert or unfocused in its larger aspects, it is here that we may observe to advantage the essentially inherent and inescapable drift towards increased organization in the modern world.

The trend towards increased organization in the thousand facets of contemporary life came about unheralded. It insinuated itself into the fabric of modern life without the polemics of philosophers or the fanfare of social prophets. Even the famous appeal of Karl Marx that workmen of all countries unite was but an answer, as he explains in the *Communist Manifesto*, to the rising organization of bourgeois society. Nor is it possible to pinpoint the origin of this trend in the edicts of some ruling class, or in the adoption of a specific social philosophy or economic policy or political program. If the organizational transformation that is encompassing the world lacks the voice of propaganda and the zeal of missionary apostles, it is because the process is at once axiomatic and inherent—it is the necessary means for the functioning of all other means in the milieu of modern life. Basically, as we have seen, organization in the field of social relations is the inherent reflection of our increasingly deliberate and conscious approach to the problems of life. The cumulative drift towards increased organization, advancing in silent compulsion, is to be traced to the same deep-seated reorientation within the delicately balanced psychic apparatus of man that had already borne fruit in his science and his machine technology. Thus it completes, in a wholly axiomatic manner, the shift in social relations from an earlier, primitive, unconscious polarity to a plane of deliberate and conscious adjustment. But if this change of direction has rewarded man with new social vistas of uncharted potential, it promises to exact a compensatory price in delimiting and constricting other aspects of his protean nature, perhaps nowhere more decisively than in the reciprocal relationships between the individual and society. For here, as we shall have occasion to note more fully, man seems destined to follow an apparently irreversible course leading to the eventual collectivization of society and the consequent atomization of the individual in a vast organizational transmutation of life. We are brought face to face with a profound challenge: the dilemma of form and content, of our traditional sense of values in a world of new form and structure. It is not merely our traditional values, but the very source of those values in a supramundane vision of life, that is threatened if not denied by ends that arise out of and reflect only the form and structure, that is to say, the means, of life. In this threatened inversion our ends will have turned into means, while our means will have become our sole ends.

II

The ineluctable nature of organization in the modern world and its universal character serve to beguile us into a wholly uncritical acceptance of its meaning, its direction, its potentialities. We feel under no obligation to question its nature or to ask whether organization, in accordance with the laws and principles of its functioning, constitutes an irreversible phenomenon in the development of society. And in failing to ask these questions we have avoided the necessity of indicating what social forces embedded in the past traditions of mankind and what essential values reborn in each individual may be counted upon to temper its momentum and direct its course. Yet these questions will prove crucial in any survey of the future condition of man, for we are entering upon a profound change of orientation in the affairs of humanity in which the silent but universal drift towards increased organization will prove not only irreversible but actually the dominant force in shaping the nature of society in the future.

Perhaps the nature of organization is most clearly comprehended in the contrast between a work of art and a machine—between an organic entity and an organized construct. Both may be said to be purposive, but while the intention of a work of art remains essentially undefined in the very degree to which it approaches its highest function, that of the machine, on the contrary, is necessarily explicit and defined, set and limited. The intention of a work of art, ranging beyond itself, is symbolic; that of a machine is strictly confined to the conscious, deliberately conceived, isolated function for which it was designed. An organic entity develops through a process of growth; an organization, however complex, through the deliberate combination and adjustment of specific means towards the attainment of specific ends. The machine is an organized assemblage of discrete parts; the work of art, an organic synthesis of its component elements. Primarily the machine is the product of intelligence, while the work of art may well have its sources in the whole substance of the human psyche. Thus the work of art involves at least in some measure an intuitive, symbolic approach to an undefined end; the machine, on the other hand, achieves a set objective through the rational solution of a defined and explicit problem. Hence the machine remains always a means, while the work of art is essentially an end in itself.

The choice of the machine as a paradigm of organization is not accidental. Historically, the rising tide of social, political, and economic organization in the modern world is directly correlated with the expansion and increasingly effective operation of our machine technology: together, they created the Industrial Revolution. The growth of modern technology and the improvement of machine design, contingent upon the phenomenal advances of science and the ingenuity of engineers, demanded in turn the development of appropriate social accommodations to insure their smooth and fruitful functioning. Thus the sustained development of our machine technology called forth a corresponding increase in organized procedures, not only in the so-called industrial countries of the West, but throughout the world. For the vast, interlocking systems of world-wide distribution of raw materials and finished products, involving the conversion of natural resources and prime energies, together with the far-flung systems of transportation and communication inherent in these complex operations, demanded an ever increasing measure of social conformity, control, and co-ordination. In time, a profound symbiosis has arisen between man and machine in which the orderly

DILEMMA OF FORM AND CONTENT

operation, the sustained control, and the predictability necessary for the efficient functioning of the machine have inevitably been reflected in an ever greater measure of social order, systematization, and organization—in a great synchronization of man and machine—affecting every aspect of human affairs. In structuring the modern world, the machine, acting as the prime crystal of organization, may be said to have initiated a self-sustaining process of crystallization that seems destined to expand into an organizational network of universal scope.

Symbolically no less than actually, this drift towards universality in the transformation of the modern world is revealed in the systematic co-ordination we have found it necessary to establish in the abstract realms of time and space. In shifting from a static to a dynamic perception of the world, we have become aware of time in a new and structural sense as an integral element of process and development, whether in the affairs of man or the routine of nature. Above all we have become aware, as never before, that time enters into every aspect of the complex transactions and intricate relationships of man in a technological world. Thus time no longer enters into life in response to the vagaries of hunger and cold or the leisurely rotation of the seasons, but in answer to the ever more miniscule adjustments demanded by a vastly expanded and infinitely complex social mechanism. The modern significance of time is attested by the universal prevalence of watches, clocks, and calendars, of timecards and timetables—the external paraphernalia and apparatus of a profound synchronization of life. With the development of world-wide and instantaneous communication, this process of synchronization was finally systematized on a global basis. Thus, in 1884, an international date line was established, and time now beats uniformly throughout the world. In a similar manner, the surface of the earth has been marked off by a definitive system of parallels of latitude and longitude, and under this Cartesian ordering of time and space a vast framework has been established for the more exact and universal co-ordination of human affairs.

In passing, it is interesting to note that proposals for rationalizing the Gregorian calendar, in use since 1582, have been considered by the Economic and Social Council of the United Nations. In a world in which the future has become an ever more integral element of the present, in which planning and prediction in the manifold aspects of modern life approach the niceties of engineering practice, the confusion of unequal months and the complex rotation of the dates of the days of the week constitute an uncouth and burdensome encumbrance. One proposal for reform calls for thirteen equal months of twenty-eight days each (with one world holiday). A "world calendar" consisting of equal quarters of three months each and one yearly world holiday has also received favorable attention. Which particular simplification of the calendar will eventually be accepted is uncertain; what is certain is that some such streamlining of the days of the year is assured. Such a gesture bears witness to the increasing unification of the world under a rationalized system of organized procedures. Nor is this trend confined solely to the conjugation, as it were, of time and space; it is evident in the effort to achieve an international language, initiated during the latter half of the nineteenth century, and it will doubtless embrace in time to come a universal reformation of our archaic number system based on the digits of our fingers and toes in favor of a duodecimal system with decisive mathematical advantages. Already, in the construction of modern electronic computers, the decimal system has been replaced by a binary number system, associated with the name of Leibnitz, which embraces infinity with nothing more than our conventional zero and the figure one.

If the basic drift towards increased co-ordination in the modern world was precipitated by the development of a machine technology, its present extension is due, in perhaps equal measure,

DILEMMA OF FORM AND CONTENT

to a principle of organizational expansion inherent in the complex functioning of modern society. However efficient a given organizational unit of operation may be when viewed separately, its ultimate efficiency will come to depend upon its smooth and unhindered functioning in respect to other phases of the social whole. We may thus say that organization in any specific area of operation tends inherently towards the elimination of chaos, uncertainty, and disorder in all contiguous enterprises of society. Hence we may enunciate the basic principle that *organization breeds organization*; like an expanding crystal field, it moves inexorably towards universality. This principle of inevitable expansion, of integration and co-ordination in every aspect of the social whole, engenders ever larger and more inclusive units of operation, until today that expansion is global in scope. For the first time in history, mankind is moving in unison, under the impetus of this trend, towards a common goal.

Needless to say, the world is not devoid of oppositional movements. But it is precisely the necessity of even such oppositional movements to organize, irrespective of their nature or purpose, in order to become effective in the modern world, that closes the circle, or perhaps it were better to say, that completes a further turn in the spiral of organized procedures. Once established, a dominant social organization constitutes a kind of gravitational field in which the form and structure of its component elements must be geared to those of the unit, the group, or society as a whole. The trend towards increased organization is universal, so that, even in democratic countries tolerant of competition and opposition, we can trace the steady convergence of dissident and conflicting elements at ever higher levels of social co-ordination. Thus we may anticipate, by way of a minor example, that the professional opposition to "socialized medicine" will eventually facilitate the very objective it is intended to forestall, if only on the general principle that the increasing organization of the constituent elements of modern society may be likened to a series of steppingstones towards its final organization. The same principle accounts for the growing dominance of the federal government and the slow but inevitable nationalization in one form or another of all major social agencies and services.

Perhaps Hitler's Germany, better than any other example in modern history, serves to illustrate, in a lurid light to be sure, the inherent necessity of organized procedures even in the pursuit of largely irrational and phantasmagorial ends. Germany's frenzied descent into the past was accompanied by all the technological advances then available, while its demoniac antirationalism, disdaining consistency, sought to establish itself by every rational means at its command. Ironically, the "blood-and-soil" revolt of Nazi Germany thus found itself committed, with characteristic Teutonic zeal and passion, to the organizational procedures of a world directed towards the future rather than the past. The Russian revolution on the other hand, free of these internal antinomies, succeeded in establishing a more permanent if not indeed more rigorous and comprehensive organizational regime than that of Germany. But this objective was of course one of its major procedural aims and accounts in part at least for the realization of its monolithic potentialities. By way of significant contrast, the inherently necessary role of organization in the modern world has been eloquently demonstrated in the complete collapse, in act as well as in thought, of nineteenth-century anarchism—the one philosophy of social cohesion that disavowed the basic postulate of deliberately established and consistently maintained organizational procedures.

In another quarter of the world, in a not altogether dissimilar orientation of human values, the spectacle of Mahatma Gandhi, seated beside his spinning wheel, bears evidence of a like, if more haunting, defeat. Gandhi's gesture, to be sure, was directed not so much against the surge and primacy of organizational procedures as such, as against the collateral effects of large-scale, modern industrialism, notably the inevitable spiritual and psychological dependence of the worker. But here too—unique as the setting was—the opposition he professed itself demanded the adoption of the same organizational methods and procedures common to other social movements, and nothing was more certain than the collapse of his protest once the magical power of his example was gone. Along with its specific economic and social objectives, Gandhi's movement had in, addition, an anti-imperialist meaning. At heart, however, it gave expression to a "way of life," a decentralized handicraft system reminiscent of William Morris' ideal scheme, in which the worker owned the tools of production and was, at least in theory if not in practice, that much closer to being the master of his fate. Nevertheless, though Gandhi won a great victory in his nonviolent opposition to British rule, he lost the equally significant struggle against the encroachment of large-scale industrialism. Under the leadership of Nehru, who may certainly be counted among his more ardent disciples, India perforce has followed the course of industrial development in unison with the rest of the modern world and in accord with the particular shibboleths of its own five-year plans. Doubtless the technological development of India was foredoomed and inevitable, and along with the world at large India is succumbing to the domination of a more aggressive, externally oriented attitude. In the face of Gandhi's inspired gesture of protest, however, this compliance with the trend of events takes on the character of a final inundation of one of the last outposts of opposition. Gandhi, the "peaceful revolutionary," was a shrewd, far-sighted, and consistent opponent whose moral principles and spiritual influence rose above the battle he lost. None the less, his spinning wheel—the emblem of a way of life—is certain to be enshrined rather than copied as India, like China, moves relentlessly into the grooves of modern industrialism, with all of its implications.

The factors and influences that tend to sustain the drift towards increased organization in the world of today and the emerging world of tomorrow are deeply and reciprocally correlated. Viewed in isolation, they seem at once cause and effect, the fruit of organization on the one hand and the seed of further organization on the other. If the smooth and efficient operation of organization depends upon an ever greater measure of predictability, for example, we may say with equal validity that predictability in the sphere of social affairs demands an ever greater measure of organization in social relations. If science in its manifold applications is in large measure responsible for our highly organized industrial civilization, industrialism, conversely, is responsible for the phenomenal expansion of applied science. This spiraling of cause and effect is the sign of a vast, encompassing movement, a universal drift. Basically, this drift represents a growing faith in the rational solution of our problems based upon our enormously increased knowledge and our scientific approach. The role of science in the transformation of the modern world, however, is by no means confined to the rise of industrialism and the establishment of our technological civilization. For the first time in the long development of mankind, we are undergoing a change of habitat, as it were, from the immediately perceived, raw actualities of nature we have shared up to now with the animal world, to the stable, continuous, and universal environment embodied in the abstract laws of nature. In adjusting ourselves, for example, to the principles and laws of electricity, whether in Borneo or Iceland, we are penetrating into a new dimension of human experience—into a deeper substratum of knowledge and awareness. But this unification on a more basic level of knowledge and experience at once invites and demands a correspondingly greater degree of mutual co-ordination and organization in all the mani-

DILEMMA OF FORM AND CONTENT 55

fold aspects of human affairs. Through science, above all through the formulated laws of nature, we establish a common foundation for the more accurate and precise comprehension of existing conditions and future eventualities. We may say, indeed, that the future of predictability—based in large measure upon these laws of nature—will in turn enhance the predictability of the future. As science enlarges our horizon, then, it conspires at the same time to increase our conscious compliance with its universally valid laws and principles; under its sovereignty our understanding of nature is being transformed, as we ourselves are being transformed, in accordance with a wholly new and inflexible dispensation.

Foremost among the dominant factors that account for the continued expansion of organizational procedures in the drift of contemporary affairs is the impressive acceleration of the world's population, previously commented upon. Like many other aspects of modern life, this startling increase is to be correlated with the rise of science and the spread of industrialism; any possible abatement in this threat will certainly involve the further application of scientific procedures. Translated into social terms, the population acceleration signifies an inevitable increase in world-wide organizational procedures of greater range and scope than any found necessary for the functioning of society in the past. Incidental to this change, if not indeed for other reasons as well, agriculture is certain to become increasingly mechanized—a transition that is slowly taking place in large areas of the world even now. A further great expansion of our machine technology in answer to the principles of automation and electronic control, as well as the even more vital factor of atomic sources of energy which alone will insure the industrialization of regions hitherto considered unavailable, seems altogether axiomatic. Finally, the persistent impact of science in every field of activity, the ever increasing demand for long-range planning and social predictability, the impending unification of the world in an ever expanding mesh of international relationships, if not indeed under a single world power—all these changes, fostering and augmenting one another, together with the basic law of organizational operation in spontaneously engendering further and ever more rigid co-ordination, suffice to suggest that the drift towards organized modes of social operation will inherently and irrevocably move towards a state of universal organization. In view of these overwhelming circumstances it seems indeed as though the form and structure of future society, functioning under the sweep of what might well be termed an *organizational determinism*, will approach ever closer to a social condition of universal collectivism.

III

Perfect organization is conceivable only on the basis of total organization. Doubtless, such a condition—however closely we may approach it—will never be fully realized. But in moving towards universal organization, we may well ask, looking into the future, what effect this direction of affairs will have upon the texture of life and the lot of man? What influence will the form and structure of society under the dominant sway of organization exert upon the means and ends, the ways and values of life? Or are we justified on the basis of our seasoned intuitions in believing after all that this drift, reaching downward into ever subtler relationships and outward into ever wider areas of human activity, represents merely the swing of the pendulum and that in due time a contrary trend will restore once more the balance between the centrifugal and the centripetal forces of the human psyche? Are we free, in short, to return at will to at least a measure of that earlier form of social cohesion, to that state of intrinsic participation which served to sustain primitive man in a condition of obedient conformity? Or again, may we envisage still another condition of life, on a higher plane, in which the freedom of the individual and the autonomy of the person are assured in a society based upon the fruitful synthesis of man's dichotomous nature? Or will man at length, conscious of his mundane failure, come to accept the vision of the mystics in seeking the integrity of the self and the brotherhood of all mankind under the divine sovereignty of God? Such a view has been maintained with profound acumen and conviction by Waldo Frank in his book, *The Rediscovery of Man*. If we reject these alternative modes of social cohesion, we seem confronted indeed by a final divergence in the functioning of society reaching to the very roots of human existence—a parting of the way in the long travail of human history and experience.

Phrasing these questions in another form, we may ask whether the freedom of the individual, the cornerstone of Western democracy, will become increasingly confined and restricted, and eventually negated, as the individual himself is reduced in status to an atom of the social mass in the progressive collectivization of society. That challenge is no longer the mere specter of literary pessimists; it is a grim reality. Hence we must face the possibility, evident in the rise of contemporary dictatorships, that the organizational structure of modern society tends implicitly to transform the reciprocal influence between individual and society, upon which in large measure the future condition of man will come to depend, into a purely unilateral relationship—the inevitable road to monolithic totalitarianism. Such an eventuality, it is to be observed, will not necessarily resemble the prescription indicated in George Orwell's novel *1984*. That picture of disastrous cruelty, power, and abasement may well reflect the crisis of a transitional phase of history but it hardly furnishes the basis for a long-range, continuous, and stable condition of human affairs. Given sufficient time, the absorption of the individual into the mass of humanity may take on an entirely different coloration, one in which the profound consciousness of individualism as a vortex of personal response and personal idiosyncrasy will have vanished, along with all its spiritual implications, to be followed by a gradually unconscious participation in the mass formulation of society as a stable, unchanging, and unchallenged unity. Cruelty and power carry in themselves the seeds of revolt against them; in the bland acceptance and adjustment of monolithic society we will have returned, on another plane, to the unquestioning acquiescence of primitive man, to a condition of the fixed and unalterable stability and permanence that have characterized, during millions of years, more than one species of biologic organisms in the perfection of their adjustment to the challenges of life. Conceivably we may return to the Garden of Eden, en masse, on pain of abandoning all knowledge of good and evil.

In view of the relative plasticity of human nature and the extraordinary range of responses man is capable of making in answer to the varied challenges of life, it would seem that he could in actuality adjust his needs to the conditions of his existence, and the conditions of his existence to his needs, with the ease and finality with which he makes such adjustments in his utopian dreams. All the elements for the solution of his problem seem at hand. Why then the halting manner, the baffling lack of an adequate and harmonious design for living? Plainly, man has been destined to suffer change, to remain in a perpetual state of transition. Having experienced a disruption in the primordial synthesis of life without being fully aware of its meaning, he has ever since found himself compelled, under the impact of his dichotomous nature, to a never ending series of changes in his protean responses to the challenges of life and nature. Each solution in turn, however, served only to sow the seeds of further problems, revealing the same challenges under new facets of his

DILEMMA OF FORM AND CONTENT

experience. Thus arose that ascending series of means, already decried by Lao-tse in the sixth century before Christ, which finally culminated in the vast machine technology of our day and behind which the more elusive and perhaps essentially indefinable ends of life must perforce recede ever further from view. Man would thus seem to have fatefully distanced himself from his erstwhile goals, and in the course of time his means, appropriating the ever enlarged foreground of his activities, inevitably usurped the position of his ends. Today man lives under a dictatorship of means more final and implacable than the overt dictatorships he fears. For in the rise of means over ends, it need hardly be emphasized, we come upon the basic necessity of organized procedures in ever wider areas of human activity, since organization itself is the indispensable means for the social functioning of all other means. Seen in this milieu, the principle of organization in the modern world takes on the character of an irrevocable determinism, an a priori law of social procedure.

In response to the sheer complexity of our endless means, we are relentlessly driven to increased order, systematization, and coordination. We are driven, in other words, to achieve greater predictability in every phase and aspect of the social fabric. Stated negatively, social organization thus demands the elimination of chaos, caprice, and uncertainty—the exclusion of all that is inchoate, spontaneous, indefinable. Stated positively, the principle of organization implies the establishment of ever greater conformity, standardization, uniformity, and regimentation—the realization of a system as explicit, defined, and concrete in respect to its ends as to its means. Hence modern society, irrespective of the particular character and structure of governments, is moving everywhere towards increased correlation and systematization of its manifold activities. And thus, throughout ever larger areas of the modern world we may perceive, in varying degrees to be sure, a profound parallelism in the basic relationship between the individual and society in which the status of the individual as such is undergoing a radical transformation—a profound convergence under the dominance of the mass. For we are entering, in a wholly new sense, a mass civilization in a collectivized world, a civilization, that is to say, in which the essential integrity and idiosyncrasy of the person is sacrificed, necessarily, to the impersonal average of the mass.

Despite their avowed difference in aims and objectives, Russia and America are basically akin by reason of the dominance of their organizational trends. What is overt and explicit in the one case is implicit and latent, to the point of being hidden, in the other. If the monolithic structure of Soviet society invited that long-range planning first introduced by Russia's five-year plans and now adopted by other countries as well, we too, beneath the beguiling remnants of our faith in individual freedom and initiative, are irredeemably following a parallel course in response to the inherent demands of our own highly complex industrial civilization. In the work of planning commissions, in the far-flung decisions of our major corporations, in the projected schemes of our more influential institutions of finance, labor, industry, research, and education, and even in the haphazard policies of our government agencies, we are moving, in piecemeal fashion it is true, towards higher levels of co-ordination and unification, and—inherently and inexorably—towards greater uniformity, standardization, and regimentation. If our course is indirect and our pace retarded, that is due in large measure to the fact that our culture, rooted in the past, functions on the basis of essentially incompatible principles: the ideal of the free individual founded on the concept of the unique and inviolate person, on the one hand, and the ethos of our wholly mechanized society which is geared always towards the arbitrary average of the mass, and therewith the implicit collectivization of society, on the other. In the silent

DILEMMA OF FORM AND CONTENT 61

clash between these incommensurate elements in our heritage, in the conflict between the social demands of the expanding mass and the traditional rights and prerogatives of the individual, we are following, less deliberately to be sure than Russia, the same path towards social conformity, unification, and co-ordination. To that end we are classified and indexed, tabulated and numbered, not as persons but as irreducible fragments of the social whole, in the name of increased efficiency and further expansion, of increased order and standardization. Our births, deaths, and marriages, our income and occupations, our personal habits, tastes, and predilections are being analyzed and correlated in a critical search for social control and predictability. Thus we are increasingly subject to statistical manipulation; everywhere graphs and percentages, vital statistics and production figures, averages and ratios, serve as the instruments of social planning and manipulation, the better to determine our statistical future and establish our statistical destiny. Plainly, in the growing tension between the individual and society, the compact, energized masses of humanity are everywhere dominant in their collective impact; and this condition of affairs, structuring the form of society through an irreversible organizational progression of varying degrees and intensities, is directed ultimately towards a state of universal compliance.

These terms have a remote and absolute ring. They may seem, indeed, like the projection of a distorted vision of our present state of affairs. Doubtless the collectivization of society is only in its incipient stages even in Soviet Russia, which boldly welcomed this approach to the future under the fatal illusion (enunciated by Engels and sustained by Lenin) that the "withering away of the state," along with the disappearance of the "dictatorship of the proletariat," would follow upon the final triumph of the revolution. Yet, however erroneous, the wishful thinking of these realists points unmistakenly to a vast historic transformation. Actually, the contribution of Russian communism in furthering the collectivization of society lies in an entirely different direction. That contribution entailed an acceptance of the means of life as its all-sufficient ends. In thus consciously and deliberately truncating the pyramid of means and ends, as it were, communism achieved at one stroke a closed system of values and a sharply focused sense of direction. Unimpeded by those ineffable and intractable elements of the human psyche which blossom forth, spontaneously and unprompted, into the higher ends of life, communism deliberately focused its efforts upon the mundane problems of collectivized survival in an age of scientific technology. Such a system of values, scrupulously limited and curtailed, necessarily tends to restrict and adjust the nature of man to the fixed patterns and arbitrary demands of society and to assimilate him within them; and in thus eliminating as far as possible the unpredictable and capricious impulses and aspirations of life, communism is but the spearhead in a general drift towards a more limited, more defined, more organized world. Russian totalitarianism, operating under a severe and relentless dictatorship, is monolithic in virtue of the stringent coalescence of its means and ends; and in this respect it is approaching, as we too are perforce approaching, the deliberate, conscious polarity of the future.

The commonly accepted notion that the freedom of the individual will be preserved, if not enhanced, as society itself becomes increasingly organized betrays our homage to nineteenth-century liberalism; today the problem of the conflict between freedom and organization is emerging in all its desperate implications as the dominant challenge of the future. The collectivization of society seems unavoidable in the modern world, and certainly our confidence in what might be described as the overriding power of deliberate optimism will not avail to solve a problem rooted in the ineradicable dichotomy of the human psyche. The complex relationship between individual and society is basically attuned to a balance of forces between our modes of social integration and our prevailing system of values. This accounts, in part at least, for the apparent reversal in the structuring of society that has characterized the course of human history. In the remote past, the behavioral patterns of primitive man did not encompass the notion of individual liberty, of individual freedom from the ethos of the tribe. On a different plane, a somewhat parallel situation obtained during much of the medieval period in Europe, and a similar absence of individualism characterized oriental civilizations throughout their history. Indeed, the idea of individualism as a philosophy of life, though not unknown to the early Greeks, is a relatively modern conception which arose and flourished, as Jacob Burckhardt has shown, only after the coming of the Renaissance. In the course of time it took on a more explicit and certainly more aggressive tone in opposition to the growing power of the state, which gradually displaced the medieval church as an authoritarian intermediary between the individual and society. Today the jurisdiction of the state, where it is not already totalitarian, threatens to become so in its gradual extension and absorption of every aspect of social existence. Thus the integration of modern society in its complex functioning is subject to the external, deliberate formulation of laws and edicts, in contrast to the virtually unconscious participation of primitive man in the ethos of the group through its customs, rites, and taboos. In either case, however, the individual as such is enmeshed in his society, consciously or unconsciously; only in the transitional interim did the concept of the free individual become a viable principle. And carrying this trend to its inherent conclusion, we cannot fail to perceive that the lingering presence of the individual in a mass society of ever greater numbers and more complex structure is doomed to diminish as the individual finally loses all status and becomes absorbed into the social body—an integral atom possessing little more than statistical existence in an expanding society.

The reversal in the structuring of society, it is plain, is a reversal in the status of the individual, but this situation is due in our day, as we have noted, to entirely different conditions from those prevailing in the life of primitive man. Indeed, in its spiritual meaning and psychological orientation, this difference sets the milieu of modern man apart, not merely from that of the remote past, but from that of his entire historic past. Devoid of the binding mores of primitive man, released from the protective panoply of religious dogma or the cultural bondage of past traditions, contemporary man finds himself reduced in stature to an ever more miniscule role in the functioning of a vast, impersonal, mass-directed civilization. Thus alienated, he is subject not only to the constraints and restrictions of society embodied in its laws, its formal codes of operation, and its departmentalized structure, but to a continuous barrage of manufactured opinion, propaganda, and mass manipulation calculated to subject him, in the last recesses of his diminished self, to the demands and conditions of his collectivized existence. The theme of the disengaged, isolated, stereotyped, and dehumanized individual, restricted at every turn to synthetic in place of organic experiences, is too worn to call for further comment. The modern individual, having attained what was previously described as the ultimate anonymity of the average, is but a shadow of the human self made opaque by the sheer density of numbers. And the zeros that express these ever expanding numbers express him too—the mechanized product of his machine technology, a being fashioned for organizational regulation and organizational manipulation.

It would be a grave misinterpretation of the trend of events, however, to believe that the ominous imbalance of modern society is basically due to the evils of dictatorship, with its concentration of power, which, overt and aggressive in one area, becomes tacitly

DILEMMA OF FORM AND CONTENT 65

accepted on defensive grounds in all contiguous areas. The "devil" theory of our historic drift is at once naïve and superficial, and its greatest danger lies precisely in the obverse theory latent in its assumptions, that a savior, galvanizing the actions of men of good will, can restore society to a state of health. Doubtless the ineradicable drift towards increased organization in the structure of modern society invites the evils of dictatorship. The rather gruesome picture of George Orwell's *1984* has unquestionably a passing validity, like yesterday's frightening headlines; but the turmoil, the cruelty, the tragic dislocations of modern life are seemingly the inevitable concomitants of the vast upheaval through which we are passing. The nature of that transformation accounts in large measure for the prevailing mood of irrational opposition, of primal refuge in emotional and instinctual release. And in that release we have seen to our horror the primitive ferocity of man appear on a global scale along side of and in contrast to the rational reconstruction of his world. Never before, it is safe to say, has mankind witnessed on so vast a scale the tragic implications, the profound opposition and inherent conflicts, of his dichotomous nature. Yet, the ultimate resolution of that opposition seems inherent and unavoidable, for we are following an orbit that subsumes the whole course of human development, in which the rise of science and the evolution of the machine are but steppingstones towards a final destination. The prevailing trend towards increased organization is seen to be rooted in a profound rational drift in the irreversible development of the human psyche; and perhaps, in view of the inescapable nature of our course, the one supreme question that remains to be asked is whether mankind, aware of the ultimate sterility of the present trends, can preserve the humanizing traditions of its vanishing past. That is indeed the supreme challenge of the future to which, in one form or another, virtually all the sensitive minds of the age have addressed themselves.

IV

We have previously observed that oppositional movements to the prevailing trend towards increased organization are obliged perforce to become themselves organized. Such movements are frustrated by a fateful circle in their procedures, compelling them to do precisely what they set out to undo. Plainly, a frontal attack upon the problem seems altogether futile; but that is merely to say the drift towards organized modes of procedure has attained a degree of dominance in its inherent necessity that is beyond challenge. The force of that drift increases cumulatively, until it may be said to generate a kind of gravitational field penetrating into the remotest recesses of our activities while encompassing ever wider areas of our existence. Meanwhile, under the continuous impact of this drift, the constructive influences of the nonrational components of the psyche have become dispersed, their power shattered, their contribution to the balance of society disrupted. These influences, once dominant in fashioning and sustaining the culture of society, can no longer be assimilated in a structured manner as in the past nor consciously absorbed and integrated into the ever more tightly woven fabric of our rational society. In this condition of essential imbalance we are compelled to rely ever more exclusively, it would seem, upon the very forces that have created the situation in which we find ourselves—upon a fateful spiraling of organizational patterns in the necessary integration of society.

At this point it may reasonably be urged that the future is compounded of possibilities beyond our knowledge, eventualities that may transform the incipient determinism spoken of above into something bearing a quite different aspect—as happened, for example, to not a few of Karl Marx's deterministic predictions. Lewis Mumford, in particular, has emphasized this point of view in our approach to the future. Calling attention to Clerk Max-

DILEMMA OF FORM AND CONTENT 67

well's doctrine of "singular points"—those unpredictable moments in the history of a system when a small force may cause an incommensurably great effect, like a spark that kindles a forest fire—he counsels us to be prepared for the rise of unpredictable personalities whose presence may change the course of events as Gandhi's did in India; or again, speaking more generally, he urges us to acknowledge the unsuspected play of forces in decisive moments of history and the emergence of unpremeditated contingencies in the routine operations and set procedures of life even in its most tranquil periods. He would challenge the assumed trajectory of our most likely probabilities with the impact of these hidden and unforeseen possibilities. And indeed, it must be granted that history, stripped of the emergent factors of the unexpected and the improbable, would hardly possess the character of high drama it has so often exhibited. The fact is indisputable: history is rich in singular points, in surprising events, in fateful personalities, in decisive inventions and crucial discoveries. Seen in larger perspective, however, the most singular and improbable events somehow fall into place, as it were, and their antecedents and consequences gradually reveal the marks of their specific deviations in the long-range trends of history. This is merely to say that history itself is the arena of vast and conflicting forces—a continuous process of far-reaching transformations during which eruptions of one or another element in the drama of events rise out of the idiom of their time to sudden triumph. The crux of the problem confronting us, however, lies precisely in the question of whether the profound dichotomy of the human psyche, which in the first place caused us to enter upon the historic phase of our development, is destined to remain permanently unresolved or whether in the course of time the conflict will be transcended in a fateful and decisive change of emphasis. It seems likely that such an eventuality, in going beyond the conflicting terrain of history as we know it, would be marked by a gradual ebbing away and disappearance of those dramatic moments that enlivened that terrain in the past. And though this eventuality may, indeed, lie in a more or less distant future, there are cogent reasons, distinct in their testimony from all previous experience, for believing that we have in fact entered upon a critical phase in the basic conflict of our psychic dichotomy. If this conclusion proves valid, we may of course still hope for the emergence of saving possibilities or of a miraculous intervention and divine redemption, as for instance in the eschatological faith of Arnold Toynbee; meanwhile, however, for us who have been denied such esoteric illuminations, a reasonable alternative would seem to be to gauge the future and take our stand upon the evidence of the inherent probabilities confronting us.

The doctrine of singular points, moreover, is open to a pessimistic interpretation no less than an optimistic one, and the solace which the argument of unpredictable possibilities offers us is equally clouded by the fact that logic, based upon our past experience, warns us to preserve a neutral attitude: in our own century, for example, at the very height of our progress, the world careened into darkness. If the thesis gains support by the inspiring example of Gandhi, it is set back conversely even further by that of Adolf Hitler. Indeed, in this febrile moment of history, the one likely singular point on the horizon is the nuclear extermination of man and all his works. The fact is that hope, like prayer, is often a measure of desperation. Joseph Conrad told an illuminating story of his examination before the Marine Department of the Board of Trade. He was asked what he would do if his ship, caught in a storm, having lost its rudder and sprung a leak, was foundering with its engines stalled. He confessed that he did not know what could be done. He stood corrected, however. At this juncture, he was informed, one could always get down on one's knees and pray to Almighty God! An attitude of hope, needless to say, is to be distinguished from one of optimism; indeed, they are often antithetical. In this sense the hope so fervently expressed in much of the critical literature concerning the future of mankind reveals our desperation rather than our optimism. Even Lewis Mumford, whose faith in man's capacity for renewal and rejuvenation is bravely optimistic, reveals the thin trace of hope upon which his sanguine attitude rests in a passage from his book, *The Conduct of Life:*

The ideas and ideals that will transform our civilization, restoring initiative to persons and delivering us from the more lethal operations of automatism, are already in existence: let me emphasize this fact. Indeed the very persons who will make the critical decisions, when a singular moment presents itself, are already, it seems probable, alive: it is even possible that a decisive change is already in operation, though as thoroughly hidden to us as the future of Christianity was to Pontius Pilate. If it were otherwise, the outlook would be black; for no change as thoroughgoing as that which will start our civilization on a new dramatic cycle can be effected overnight.

One cannot quarrel with the hope expressed in this passage, however much one may question its optimism; but in any case such attitudes somehow cancel each other, leaving us with an outlook that is bleak and gray, if not indeed black, as Mumford says. It is true we have reached a historic moment of high critical significance, a moment of profound challenge; but this fact in itself gives no assurance that an effective countervailing movement, capable of turning the tide of events, is certain to arise. On the contrary, there are ominous signs on the horizon which would seem to indicate that such a reaction is no longer feasible and that we may already have arrived at a point of no return in our journey towards ultimate mechanization and automation and our headlong drift towards universal organization.

The growing body of writing concerned with the future condition of mankind has blossomed forth in our day into a new and significant literary genre. However speculative, the challenge of the future is presented most often in terms of some vital and profound choice, followed by a dubious abundance of critical advice, analysis, exhortation, and prognosis. There appear to be innumerable schools of thought and opinion on the subject—political, social, economic, religious, educational, and scientific—and to each the future welfare of humanity is contingent, it would seem, upon some crucial *if* that serves as the key to our salvation. Plainly, the problem has endless aspects: it is at once personal and international, spiritual and social, psychological and ideological, individual and collective. With this bewildering complexity of approaches, it would seem that each solution could have at best only a partial validity. The recurrent *if*s lodged in each solution are like a series of archways revealing a resplendent future, each after its own fashion. But in their ensemble effect—like the continuous archways in the paintings of Chirico—they suggest rather a blind state of negation and frustration. We seem consigned to an endless series of ambiguous vistas and futile choices.

In the passage quoted above, for example, it is apparent that Mr. Mumford's reassuring words take little account of a characteristic dilemma in our approach to the future. If the dominant drift towards organized procedures results in a greater measure of mechanization and automation, that drift tends likewise to eliminate free individuals as such—"the very persons who will make the critical decisions when a singular moment presents itself." As the probabilities favoring a continuation and acceleration of this drift increase, the possibilities adverse to such a drift will inherently decrease; in short, the incidence of both singular points and the persons likely to transmute them into paths of world salvation will inevitably diminish. We are in a cul-de-sac. The prevailing world drift towards organization seems, even now, overwhelming, and though the meshes of organization remain sufficiently open, here and there, to permit occasional gestures of a contrary nature to arise, these ripen at best into isolated and ephemeral enterprises, destined to be reabsorbed, sooner or later, into the organized fabric of society. The communitarian movements of France and Italy, commented upon at length in Erich Kahler's book *The Tower and the Abyss*, are as he himself says, oases and islands in an alien world. Like the small communities of primitive man or the relatively limited religious communities of America, their vitality arises out of the organic nature of their missions or ways of life, but these in turn are contingent upon the possibility of direct personal communication between all their members. Hence such movements, in their very nature, are self-limiting and, like the Amana Colony of Iowa, for example, are destined to succumb in time to the impingements of contrary social forces. The hope of establishing countervailing movements is not without a poignant appeal, but the preponderant impact of mass organizations impedes and finally destroys their influence, where indeed it does not prevent their occurrence in the first place, as in Soviet Russia and other dictatorial countries.

If this is the general fate of social oases sustained by intense communal ideals, plainly the same corrosive forces are even more effective in the case of the isolated individual. We are all subject in our public behavior, whatever our private response, to influences beyond our control. Moreover, the forces of social conformity are constantly augmented, refined, and expanded. In the pervasive atmosphere of our organized milieu, the individual as such is subject to the coercive forces of social conditioning in the very degree to which he would oppose them. Hence, by the calculus of probabilities we may anticipate a steady curtailment in the freedom of the individual as the collective mass of society increases its power and domination. Historically, the transitional stage of individualism, arising out of a welter of changing modes of social cohesion, is past. And, turning toward the future, we can already perceive in the final eclipse of the individual the more arid and uniform conditions of a new milieu—the plateau stage of modern collectivism.

All that has been said concerning the fate of the individual or the isolated social experiment in the milieu of the modern world applies with equal force, on a somewhat more gradual basis to be sure, to the spirit and institution of nationalism. During the past hundred years nationalism has flared up with varying degrees of intensity in one country after another from Bismarck's Germany and Mazzini's Italy to modern Africa. At the same time, a closer interrelationship has arisen between nations—a significant movement towards internationalism. These movements, though they operate on different levels, seem related contrapuntally, as it were, as though nationalism were indeed a defensive measure, an intuitive presentiment of an overriding internationalism. In this connection, it is not without meaning that we speak on the one hand of national passions and on the other of international planning—the one emotionally oriented, the other rationally. If the relationship between these principles has the appearance of an opposition, actually it represents the transcendence of one form of social order and cohesion by another more inclusive form under the prevailing world-wide compulsion towards increased organization. We are caught, then, in a universal stream of change in which even oppositional movements, whether on the scale of the person or the nation, are paradoxically swept along in a vast, unilateral, and all-inclusive drift.

Today the zenith of state power has been achieved under totalitarian dictatorship. This phenomenon is due in large measure

DILEMMA OF FORM AND CONTENT

to the fact that the state attains maximum power under the conditions of war—an observation made long ago by Randolph Bourne, who spoke of war as "the health of the State." Dictatorial governments are forced at all times, however, to maintain a condition of war—primarily against their own peoples, considered as individuals, under the pious plea of maintaining collective welfare, and secondarily against other nations, as a "cold war" of limited aggression between periods of actual conflict. Democratically constituted governments approach a similar degree of organizational absolutism only during active warfare. Nevertheless, the pattern of the cold war has rapidly infected the morale of democratic states as well, and universal, peacetime conscription, along with other elaborate military, economic, and industrial preparations for war, is but a reflection of the sharp tightening of state control and state mobilization characteristic of the more advanced totalitarian powers. As a consequence of this ruthless competition, international war looms as the most imminent and ominous threat confronting mankind today. Yet, by a curious paradox, the logic of nuclear war may hasten international agreements having as their purpose the eventual negation of war and the threat of war, as least on an international scale. But the spirit, pattern, and technique of military morale and group discipline, we may be certain, will remain to inspire a proper sense of fear and power among the civilian population of dictatorial states, while behind the façade of our own humanistic goals and democratic procedures, we too will perpetuate, without perhaps fully comprehending our actions, the psychological if not military regimentation in a common movement towards the increased collectivization of society. The persistent threat of war has merely energized a trend inherent in the logic of events.

While the collectivization of society is implicit in all totalitarian regimes, whether to the left or the right, collectivization itself is rooted in the slow, inevitable conversion of the form and structure of human society under the compulsion of a unique symbiosis between man and machine, in the fearful multiplication of the human species with its inherent pressure upon our natural resources, and in the implicit dominance of rational rather than instinctual modes of operation and procedure in an ever more complex and interrelated world. These fateful factors possess a drama of their own, but it is not so much the drama of transient events, however disturbing, as that of the silent and implacable forces at the base of our civilization. Mankind is passing through a structural metamorphosis in which the form of society, fashioned by its means, techniques, and procedures, is gradually determining its aims and ends, its values and attitudes, its essential orientation. This condition of affairs, we have seen, follows upon the fact that man can no longer meet the complex urgencies of life without the aid of organized procedures, and having entered upon this approach to the challenges of life, he cannot reverse his course or live half in the future and half in the past by revitalizing the simplicities of an earlier dispensation. In this sense it may indeed be said that the destiny of mankind is conditioned by an ineluctable determinism.

Man cannot deliberately forgo the conscious advances he has achieved in the course of his long development, for human history, like other organic processes—indeed like organic evolution in general—necessarily follows an irreversible path. Needless to say, our present civilization may degenerate and collapse as other civilizations have in the past; but such a contingency is not to be identified with a devolution along the course of our former evolution. In respect to the dichotomous nature of the human psyche, this is merely to say that man cannot voluntarily restore the erstwhile supremacy of the instincts as guiding principles of life—and least of all can he do so through the agency of intelligence! If society in our day is subject to a decisive imbalance owing essentially to the dominance of man's rationality, he can

DILEMMA OF FORM AND CONTENT

only hope to regain the unstable equilibrium of his former condition not by a Rousseauesque return to primitive life, but by the exercise on a new and different level of a sagacity limited at best to a few poets, mystics, and seers. To attempt to regain such an equilibrium socially is to fly in the face of an overwhelming development, anchored in the vast technological apparatus of mankind—a feat accomplished by the legendary Erewhonians of Samuel Butler, but without equivalent in the annals of history. Immured in a profound crisis, we seem to be only vaguely aware of the fateful dilemma of form and content in which we find ourselves. That our society has reached a climactic imbalance is hardly open to question. That this imbalance is due, however, to a final parting of the way between the influences of instinct and intelligence in the historic development of mankind seems to some of us improbable if not meaningless. We are accustomed, in the first place, to think of the cultural development of man as the fruit of a coalescence, a creative synthesis of all his psychic faculties, tinctured by time and events into the varied patterns of his multi-dimensioned history. Like the idea of progress, this mode of development seems to us inherent and axiomatic. In the second place, we tend to believe that we are the masters of our fate, capable of shifting the emphasis in the spectrum of our values in response to our wisdom and insight, our knowledge and intelligence. And though we are prepared to grant that man in his freedom may conceivably fail to achieve his full potentialities, we do not recognize that he can be deprived of that basic freedom which constitutes his supreme endowment. In harmony with this faith, we are convinced that the pendulum marking his response to the challenges of life will never remain poised at some tangential angle and the drama of the conflict that has marked history in the past will never cease as man achieves ever new transformations and new interpretations in the endless play of his psychic forces. The destiny of mankind will remain inscrutable if only because it will forever change.

Lewis Mumford, in his admirable book, *The Transformations of Man*, has traced for us in clear outline the basic ebb and flow of man's changing status since he first diverged from the biologic hierarchy. In these transformations man is seen to oscillate, on an ever higher and more complex plane, between his intuitive, instinctual responses and his spiritual perceptions on the one hand, and his rational reactions to the varied challenges of life on the other. If, in our day, his machine technology, his scientific progress, and his all-encompassing extroversion have carried him far in one direction, it seems reasonable to believe, on the basis of his past fluctuations, that he is destined, sooner or later, to enter a dark night of the rebirth and regeneration of yet another transformation that will affirm once again the values and ideals of a more balanced humanity. To interpret our present imbalance as permanent is to put an end to this spiritual tension, to envisage a turning point in the history of mankind more decisive and more profound than any in the past. Indeed, it is to look upon history itself as a brief interregnum, a moment of febrile transition between long ages reaching towards the remote past in one direction and an unknown future of ever less tension and ever less change in the other. Actually, as we have seen, there are cogent reasons for believing that history may have but a transitional meaning and that the processes which account for its seething drama may also account, under a different disposition of its component forces, for a cessation of that drama. Conceivably, in the imbalance of our present moment mankind may have passed the apogee of its highest ferment, its greatest activity, and having passed, as it were, the high point of a watershed, is now destined to move towards a state of increasing fixity, permanence, and stability.

The validity of such an interpretation comes to depend, in any final analysis, upon the assumption that the dominance of intelligence will become validated in an irreversible triumph. The modern world has indeed placed its highest faith precisely in the pragmatic successes of intelligence; it remains to be seen whether these high hopes will be justified by a progressive amelioration of man's condition, or whether in turn, intelligence, too, has its own inherent limitations, its own ineradicable confines.

CHAPTER 3

Challenge of Intelligence

I

THE ABSENCE of a machine technology in the ancient world of Greece and Rome, of China, India, and Egypt, is at once baffling and revealing. Whatever the explanation, including the obvious lack of a sustained scientific tradition, the absence of a machine technology in these highly developed societies cannot be ascribed to a want of intelligence. Their early mathematical attainments and profound cultural achievements make any such assumption untenable and meaningless. Plainly, the sum total of human knowledge at the time and the scientific discipline necessary to sustain its effective manipulation were inadequate for the purpose. But more important, intelligence itself was otherwise directed. As Erich Kahler has pointed out, doubtless this was in large measure due to the overriding influence of religious attitudes, which placed man and nature in a fixed and divine order. Not until the coming of the Renaissance was Western man prepared to indulge his intellectual faculties in a new and more searching approach to nature—an approach that blossomed forth, in a few short centuries, into modern science and the technological transformation of the world. Viewed in this historic context, the long-delayed application of intelligence to a systematic scrutiny of the world about us reveals its essential dependency upon other factors in the psychic make-up of man; indeed, seen in this light, it would appear that intelligence per se is directionless, a neutral agency of the mind concerned above all with the mutual relationships of presented facts and given data. Thus knowledge, in its cumulative aspects, is seen to act as a moving fulcrum for the ever increasing power and dominance of intelligence in the growing complexity of human affairs; and the high status of intelligence in the modern world is but a reflection of its indispensability in an era of ever more precise and extended factual information and knowledge.

But the obverse of this statement is at least equally pertinent: the application of intelligence to the teeming world about us has vastly extended our store of established facts and immeasurably enhanced our knowledge of nature. This advance is the fruit above all of the scientific method. That method, however, as P. W. Bridgman has said, is but a special case of the method of intelligence itself, and, as he was careful to observe in *Reflections of a Physicist*, "any apparently unique characteristics (in the field of science) are to be explained by the nature of the subject matter rather than ascribed to the method itself." Recognizing this fact, we have come to look upon knowledge and intelligence in their mutual interaction as the key to further progress, and, encouraged by the phenomenal advances of the past few centuries, we have acquired a virtually unbounded faith in their potency. Indeed, the triumphs of the scientific method have placed an aura about human intelligence as a unique and potentially limitless faculty of the mind, and certainly today no prognostication or exhortation concerning the future of mankind fails to emphasize the critical role of intelligence in the further enhancement of human existence. Thus, for example, G. G. Simpson in his searching treatise, *The Meaning of Evolution*, says, "Probably the new character most surely necessary for evolution beyond the present limits is an increase in intelligence above the existing maximum. Human progress depends upon knowledge and learning, and the capacity for these is conditioned by intelligence." The pronouncement is sufficiently typical in its emphasis upon the unique character and unique role of intelligence to stand by itself. The development of human intelligence, achieved in the future, perhaps, by genetic manipulation, as well as through the more traditional modes of educational training and discipline, seems to our scientifically minded, technologically advanced generation the one open-sesame to assured progress and advancement. Human intelligence is looked upon, in fact, as the keystone of that far-reaching psycho-social development which Julian Huxley considers the only possible avenue to any further major transformation or evolutionary advance—not only for man, but for the whole biologic hierarchy. In short, whatever sense of limitation or inadequacy we may harbor with respect to human intelligence at present, we are convinced, it would seem, if only on the basis of our tangible progress of the past, of its virtually inexhaustible potentialities for the future.

Moreover, the advances we hopefully anticipate are not contingent solely upon the further organic development of our complex brain mechanism. In this sense, there appears to have been little or no evolutionary progress since long before man became a historic being. Even the results of future genetic manipulation promise to remain at best uncertain, slow, and highly exacting in the sustained controls and subtle interpretations of values demanded over extended periods of time. On the other hand, the brain, like the muscles of the body, may well be susceptible of mechanical "amplification," as W. R. Ashby has shown. In restricted areas this extension of the frontiers of intelligence has already been attained by high-speed electronic computers; and here we have perhaps only achieved an initial breakthrough in a domain of unsuspected possibilities. At present, however, it seems highly questionable whether the principles of selection upon which the operation of so-called "intelligence amplifiers" are based will prove valid in the case of problems involving less than explicit answers. And this question, in turn, touches upon the true scope and nature of intelligence: its definition, its limitations, its meaning, and above all upon the crucial distinctions to be made between intelligence, on the one hand, and judgment, understanding, and wisdom (to use an obsolete term that is knocking on the door of modern consciousness), on the other hand.

Meanwhile, the cumulative nature of human knowledge, which has long since resulted in a social deposit of fact and information utterly beyond the range and capacity of any individual, is certain to sustain its effective expansion. Thus, while the sheer growth of human knowledge seems assured, its meaningful synthesis, its ultimate disposition and arrangement appear increasingly elusive, as though we were involved here in a kind of Malthusian dilemma. Though knowledge increases in an ever expanding progression, our ability to absorb and assimilate it seems destined to remain relatively stationary, and, in this sphere too, mankind approaches an implicit "perimeter of the future" spoken of in a previous chapter. A sense of this situation may be obtained from the simple observation that, while a representative library is likely to contain several hundred thousand volumes, few individuals are to be credited with the authorship of more than a score of them, while even the reading of such rare individuals throughout their lifetimes is certain to be limited to the merest fraction of the whole. Human knowledge has grown into a vast, socially inherited, and socially sustained agglomeration—a reservoir of incalculable individual contributions that never ceases to expand and in which even the rejected errors of the past remain to serve as negative signposts, as it were, to the future. Now, this immense mass of fact, knowledge, and experience may in time become synthesized and correlated beyond our own powers through the agency—let us assume—of subtly devised mechanisms, but for the moment such a hope seems altogether improbable and meaningless. Thus intelligence, dependent upon the expanding mass of human knowledge and information as a fulcrum, may in time become hampered and ultimately frustrated by an inherently fateful predicament. Collectively knowing always more than he can individually absorb and comprehend, man may conceivably lose his way in the complex galleries of some future Tower of Babel.

In our time the synthesis of the diverse disciplines of science presents a staggering problem, and the synthesis of all knowledge seems a utopian ideal. Nevertheless, we have of course achieved fantastic advances in the sciences as well as in technology, and if these achievements are the fruit of human intelligence nothing would seem more reasonable than to anticipate their continued rise and the further nurture and enhancement of that intelligence. The emphasis upon a *rational* approach to the solution of our problems would thus appear altogether persuasive, and perhaps the nineteenth-century dream of inevitable progress would have seemed validated but for the course of events in the twentieth, accompanied as it was by a gnawing sense of an inward hiatus, a profound rift, somewhere in the fabric of modern life. Much has been written about the nature of that rift. Possibly the day is not sufficiently advanced to reveal its character in full; meanwhile, the extraordinary burgeoning of psychological insight and research following upon the initial contributions of Sigmund Freud would seem to suggest that the nature of the rift is basically psychic. Looking at the grievous travail of our century, it would seem that, in their very moment of triumph, the dominantly rational approaches to the challenges of life had infused the more primary, instinctual forces of the human psyche with renewed vitality; like a conflagration, the irrationality of man broke forth in a demonic tumult of world wars and world cruelties of unprecedented ferocity and magnitude, while his spirit, seeking surcease in the paradoxes of Existentialism or Zen Buddhism, or in the sweeping revolt of the arts, or more commonly in the feeble stance of institutionalized religion, was in fact adrift in an utter maze of relativity. We are caught, it is apparent, in a vortex of conflicting forces in which the dichotomous structure of the human psyche is being strained as never before.

However resourceful intelligence may have proved itself in meeting the challenges of external nature, it appears somehow less than adequate in meeting the challenges of our own inward nature. Perhaps that is not its proper domain, as Henri Bergson implied in asserting that intelligence was primarily geared to function within the wholly objective realm of the material world. In casting accounts, we seem confronted by a twofold limitation in the scope and nature of intelligence. On the one hand, as we have noted, operating as a correlating or organizing agency of the mind devoted above all to the relationships of the parts of an ensemble rather than to a vision of the whole, intelligence appears at a loss in coping with the totality of human knowledge to which it inevitably contributes—a situation that promises to become in time far more pressing and ambiguous than we are at present inclined to grant. But this inherent limitation of intelligence has a bearing in general upon the deeper and more inclusive aspects of life, leaving us adrift in respect to the more ultimate meaning even of our technology and science—fields in which intelligence plays a dominant role. Intelligence is a pragmatic faculty of the mind, moving naturally within the locus of established values and concepts. It rarely encompasses the scene as a whole or serves as the impetus for enlarging the realm of ideas or penetrating into the significance of our values; that is more likely the task of our imagination, our intuition and wisdom. On the other hand, in respect to the baffling dilemmas and challenges of our inward selves, intelligence per se appears even more limited and sterile, impassive and remote, in its essentially mechanistic stratagems and rationalistic procedures. Modern psychology has amply demonstrated the virtual impotence—or perhaps it would be better to say incompatibility—of intelligence in the realm of our emotional and psychic responses. If the scientifically minded humanists of the nineteenth century, as they do in our own, looked upon intelligence without reservations, it is now seen to have limiting aspects that are certain to shadow in some degree the sanguine vision of its triumphant sway in the future. For, like other facets of the human psyche, intelligence is not without its own inherent confines, its own restrictive boundaries.

There is, moreover, a further ambivalent aspect of intelligence that we are inclined to overlook in our wholehearted faith in its axiomatic beneficence. The uses of intelligence attained an entirely new dimension with the rise of science. Increasingly, mankind learned through the agency of science to adapt itself to the formulated laws of nature, rather than, as in the past, to nature directly. But this radical accomplishment, involving the development of our highly complex technology, resulted in a progressive differentiation and specialization of human activities, until in our day the individual finds himself perforce isolated in a minimal capacity on the edge of ever vaster, socially sustained enterprises. The characteristic dependency and relative insignificance of the individual in the intricate functioning of our modern technological apparatus was unwittingly demonstrated, and not without somber implications, during the last war, as a result of the secrecy attending the production of the original atomic bomb. Whereas this enterprise involved well over a hundred thousand people, not more than a score or two, it is safe to say, actually knew or understood what was being accomplished. The innocence of the remainder about the nature of the enterprise in no way affected its success. And, in a similar sense, our individual relationship to the

CHALLENGE OF INTELLIGENCE 85

technological system as a whole is necessarily partial and vicarious, necessarily remote and inconsequential. As the technological system expands in scope and complexity, the role of the individual becomes correspondingly insignificant, until finally he is reduced to a mere cog in a scheme of things he neither controls nor understands. The benefits of intelligence in this dominant sphere of life are thus seen to have a cumulative social meaning of far-reaching but ultimately fateful consequence. The functioning of the system, aided increasingly by automation, acts—certainly by no malicious intent—as a channel of intelligence, by which the relatively minute individual contributions of engineers, inventors, and scientists eventually create a reservoir of established knowledge and procedure no individual can possibly encompass. Thus man appears to have surpassed himself, and indeed in a certain sense he has. Paradoxically, however, in respect to the system as a whole, each individual becomes perforce an unthinking beneficiary—the mindless recipient of a socially established milieu. Hence we speak, not without justification, of a push-button civilization—a system of things devised by intelligence for the progressive elimination of intelligence! That is to say, the operations of the social mass under the impact of our technology continually delimit the need of individually directed responses, and the autonomous functioning of the system approaches an ideal of frictionless efficiency in the degree to which it serves the demands of human automatons. But this situation harbors a fateful truism: the consolidation of the mass and the extrusion of the individual are obverse sides of the same coin.

Seen from this point of view, it is at once apparent why the operation of our modern technological apparatus demands an ever increasing measure of social organization and social control. Moreover, this drift is inherent and inescapable, and it operates irrespective of the particular economic or political milieu in which the system is functioning. The extreme mechanization of modern life moves inherently towards social collectivization, and this overriding condition of modern existence explains the frequently striking parallelism in the social trends of otherwise alien modes of governmental operation. It explains the often surprising similarities in the functioning of American capitalism and Russian communism, or again the common drift beneath the awakening and transformation of the recently primitive cultures that have now assumed the garb and idiom of contemporary society. The organizational impact of modern technology, evident throughout the world, has a common, unifying aspect. And, however indirectly, it is universally an index and measure of the social rather than the individual operations of intelligence in the direction of human affairs. But that is merely to say modern social organization serves to define the role of the individual and to determine the locus of his activities on the basis of the social intelligence of the community in general, in place of his own individual intelligence; thus the freedom of the individual becomes increasingly circumscribed, not as in primitive society by the shared mores and customs of the tribe, but by the arbitrary mandates of a system that is intricately complex beyond his scope. And having entered upon this scheme of things, society finds itself compelled to advance along the orbit of its adopted path. In this way organization, as we have noted earlier, breeds organization by an inherent law of its functioning, until the process, having passed a point of no return, leads by one track or another to the ultimate collectivization of society.

In the actual functioning of our technological world we are becoming aware of unsuspected strains and stresses, of new and unfamiliar contingencies. Even the operations of intelligence, running counter to our more sanguine expectations, are seen to harbor a threat that has not gone unnoticed or unanswered. Thus Lewis Mumford, conscious of this threat, has observed in *The Transformations of Man* that one of the functions of intelligence "is to take account of the dangers that come from trusting solely to intelligence." Unfortunately, the laxness of this comment is somewhat obscured by the neatness of its phrasing. It is not within the province of intelligence to evaluate the limits of its functions; that is the task of our understanding, our imagination and wisdom, our judgment. But in this distinction, which may well appear at first glance merely a matter of semantics, we touch upon a profound dilemma in the texture of modern life. While the sway and influence of intelligence deeply affect the social fabric of life, transforming the world utterly beyond the capacities and powers of the individual, he in turn remains isolated within the locus of his personal comprehension and judgment, his own limited wisdom and understanding. Anxious and uncertain, or more likely heedless and resigned, he finds himself, along with everyone else, regimented in a world of towering accomplishments and well-nigh superhuman achievements. Under these circumstances, it is small wonder that he welcomes, not infrequently with a spurious if compelling sense of personal freedom, the vast organizational network of modern life which serves to guide and sustain, to control and direct him at every turn. And by way of contrast, the occasional iconoclast who would disentangle the complex strands of this dilemma soon finds himself reduced to silent impotence in the overwhelming maelstrom of the social system. Thus the stray insight and wisdom of the individual become at best futile wisps in the overriding momentum of an ever more highly organized, technologically directed society. Increasingly, our private sagacity lies at the mercy of our cumulative social intelligence. The collectivization of society, inherent in our technological development, constitutes a rising barrier which the individual will be unable to surmount as he himself, with whatever insight and wisdom he may command, vanishes from the scene.

We are at the moment, here in America, in the preliminary

phases of this impending drama. Traditionally our culture was built upon the ideal of individual freedom; meanwhile, we have contributed perhaps more than any other nation to the development of that high system of technological procedures which threatens, inherently and inevitably, the freedom of the individual. By and large, we have stoutly refused to acknowledge the challenge of this situation, despite the warnings and appeals of social-minded writers, philosophers, and psychologists, who have urged us to stem the tide and alter the drift of affairs. Inspired by a humanistic faith in the spiritual primacy of freedom, our growing literature of analysis, protest, and persuasion testifies to the mounting urgency of the problem and incidentally to our deep-seated belief in the traditional prerogatives of the individual under a free-enterprise system. In harmony with these suppositions, we are inclined to see our conflicts and dilemmas in moral terms of personal adjustment, and our literature of inquiry and protest, strengthening this interpretation, consists largely of hortatory appeals and moral diatribes. Perceiving neither the depth and magnitude of the problem nor its inner meaning, our critical inquiries end all too often with the consoling thought that of course "it will not happen here." Meanwhile, it is happening. The structure of society, even in America, is undergoing a subtle transformation, as Archibald MacLeish pointed out in noting that the nation is becoming a concept spelled with a capital *N* on its way to emerging as the "sovereign state." That is to say, we too, as the Russians, are succumbing to the overriding dictates of centralized organization in the complex functioning of our affairs. But this is merely to underscore, in turn, the dominant influence of our socially circumscribed intelligence in its basic conflict with our deeper, intransigent wisdom. In that conflict, as we have seen, the issue is set not in the moral terms of our individual consciences —however valid in isolated cases—but in the overwhelming sway of an encompassing technological milieu in a world of increasing population and decreasing resources. Irrespective of our ideals, our faiths, our traditions, we are moving, it is clear, towards a world of collectivized social enterprise.

The drift towards increased collectivization follows upon the social necessity of large-scale planning. Our era, which has been burdened with many epithets, might well be called the "age of planning," since we have never before faced the future more deliberately and consciously in terms of long-range social enterprises and far-flung schemes of technological development. Indeed, we find ourselves confronted with the necessity of "inventing the future," in the apt phrase of Dennis Gabor. But here again we come upon a parting of the way, upon a harassing dilemma in our social outlook. In the very degree to which we set the form and pattern of our future milieu and define the locus of our behavior, we are establishing the framework of coming events and therewith the more exact predictability of the future. Plainly, the higher functioning of our technology demands an ever increasing measure of predictability, not only in the technological apparatus, but in man himself; and as the momentum of the system increases, it invades progressively greater areas of the uncommitted future. Thus it sets boundaries to our course and limits the future freedom of individual and society alike. In place of the established milieu of habit and custom prevailing in the past, we are engineering the patterns of the future on the basis of our rational planning and the projected demands of our technological scheme of things. This drift of affairs, however, appears to us inherent and unavoidable—an axiomatic course of events; and perhaps only in retrospect are we inclined to count its costs in the slow attrition between individual and society revealed by our emerging collectivization. This eventuality was commented upon long ago by Freud in his *Civilization and Its Discontents* with the curt observation that "it almost seems as if humanity could be united into one great whole if there were no need to trouble about the happiness of individuals." Under communism, this truncated condition of affairs is welcomed in the name of freedom; but that attitude is perhaps no more illusory than our own commonly accepted prescription for avoiding the ills of planning—advocated for instance by Karl Mannheim—by the simple device of planning for freedom! Thus we would answer the dilemma of our future freedom by calling for an expansion of intelligence, trusting to our deliberate maneuvers to curb its essential attributes. But this seemingly bold solution is not unlike spinning the wheels of a car already mired. In brief, our homeopathic approach to the problem, while deepening our dilemma, leaves our faith and hope in intelligence more sacrosanct than ever. In the spreading travail of our world we seem desperately anxious to avoid the possibility that our axiomatic belief in the unqualified efficacy of intelligence may itself be open to question. To do otherwise would be to throw the problem back into the hands of the individual at the very moment when he is vanishing behind the horizon of a collectivized society.

II

The temper of the times, however, is not wholly devoid of countervailing movements. Beginning with the protest of eighteenth- and nineteenth-century Romanticism, these movements of intuitive immediacy are to be recognized today in the brash revolt of contemporary art, on the one hand, and in the widespread retreat on the other towards the pious gestures of the past implicit in our rampant anti-intellectualism and even more rampant antirationalism. It would almost seem, as William Barrett suggests in his book, *Irrational Man,* that the ancient Furies have returned to demand their due of modern man by playing upon his psychic imbalance in an age dedicated to scientific empiricism and the rational organization of the secular world. And indeed,

CHALLENGE OF INTELLIGENCE

has not science itself revealed significant fissures in its rational structure that presage the emergence of fateful "perimeters of the future" to hedge its once limitless dreams: Heisenberg's principle of indeterminacy; Bohr's principle of complimentarity; and perhaps most significant of all, Gödel's demonstration of certain inherent limitations in the very structure of mathematics? Nor can we pass by as merely accidental and irrelevant the fact that the significant advances in psychological theory and research happen to have coincided with a period of wholly exceptional and profound psychic unrest. Patently, beneath the surface of events there are signs of uneasy revolt, of a retreat into the latent realm of the unconscious—into the primordial reservoir of feeling, instinct, and intuition. Nor dare we forget that in our day the demonic irrationality of man reached its beastly apex precisely in a Germany that stood close to the forefront of contemporary civilization. The implications of that disaster are terrifying in the grim shadows they cast upon the modern world at large.

Our psychic imbalance is more drastic than we dare admit. And beyond the impact of this dichotomous situation, we are subject to a pervasive relativism in respect to the standards and values of life that hangs like a mist over the metaphysical void of modern existence. Thus adrift, we are more inclined than ever to run to extremes in our effort to allay the strain and stress of an imbalance we sense without critical comprehension and a relativism we accept without conviction. In this confused and ambiguous atmosphere, we place our faith and hope in quite contrary modes of salvation: on the one hand, we believe our present dilemmas and ambiguities will vanish in time under the continued sway of our scientific rationalism and, on the other hand, we would right our imbalance by deliberately curtailing, if not disavowing, the scientific rationalism we conceive to be its cause. The parallelogram of involved forces is thereby reduced to a flat and fruitless opposition whose sterility, moreover, is buried beneath the dominating momentum of our technological commitments. For despite the tensions and uncertainties of our situation we are irrevocably set upon a course dictated by the demands and commitments of our triumphant technology, which rises, supreme and unaffected, above the clash of our ideologies. In these circumstances the sweeping relativism of the age would seem to demand a pragmatic approach to the solution of our problems; but that is merely to say we are irredeemably concerned with the means of life rather than its ends in facing the challenge of the future.

Indeed, under the impact of our mechanistic triumphs it would almost seem that we had come to believe that the unresolved dilemmas of contemporary life and civilization were themselves essentially mechanical in nature, subject to a mechanical solution within easy reach of our collective intelligence, if not the faltering light of our individual wisdom. Viewed in this perspective, our means will inevitably come to dominate and determine our ends and by this collective sleight of mind insure our optimistic approach to the future. Above all, we confidently resign ourselves by this stratagem to the operations of an intelligence whose special province lies precisely in the manipulation and organization of the means of life. Thus insulated, as it were, intelligence comes to be accepted as the sovereign, indeed the sole, agency of the human psyche appropriate to the structural ordering of our present milieu in anticipation of the demands and challenges of the future. The consequence of this one-sided emphasis, however, is to increase rather than decrease the very imbalance now threatening us.

At the risk of seeming to harbor an antirational and anti-intellectual attitude in the perennial fashioning of our values, it becomes necessary to examine more closely the functioning of intelligence in its increasingly isolated dominance. Before proceeding with this task, it may be well, however, to emphasize once again the essentially collective character and cumulative

CHALLENGE OF INTELLIGENCE 93

nature of its social influence. The problem before us is not concerned with any rise in the intelligence quotient of the modern individual in comparison with his forebears, recent or remote, if only because there appears to be no evidence, according to historians and anthropologists, for believing that any perceptible change has occurred. On the contrary, though our knowledge has advanced, our intelligence in its individual potency has apparently remained unchanged since long before recorded history. But therein we come upon the crux of a modern dilemma. Despite the relative fixity of human intelligence, we seem destined to follow an ascending course of ever increasing complexity and involvement in a world which, even now, appears wholly incommensurate with our individual comprehension and individual capacities. Doubtless we may still embrace the world of our fashioning in terms of general principles, but the detailed structure and precise functioning of that world in all its far-flung operations demand an altogether superhuman comprehension and understanding. As individuals, we thus find ourselves on the periphery of an ever expanding circle—remote and isolated on the fringes of a system in which perforce we have our being and draw our sustenance. As a consequence, a corrosive sense of "alienation"—a feeling at once of anxiety and ennui—has become the psychological hallmark of modern man. He finds himself reduced at every turn to a vicarious participation in an ever more recondite and complex system of things, in which the range of his perceptions, experience, and intelligence is hopelessly outdistanced by the collective achievements of society at large. The intricate functioning of that society comes to depend not only upon the organized relationships of contributions from the varied disciplines of science—from physics, chemistry, mathematics, biology, geology, psychology—but also upon the involved procedures of business, industry, commerce, mining, agriculture, transportation, and communication, upon the complex legacies of law and history, upon a vast multitude of minute and intangible assets beyond all calculation. And as the social body, in response to the inherent demands of its functioning, grows more compact and highly organized, the individuals composing it experience a progressive diminution in status, since they in turn must adjust themselves, under the silent coercion of events beyond their control, to the collective demands and collective procedures of society. Unimpeded, intelligence hastens this process of conversion in which the organization of the means of life becomes the primary condition of its sustained and complex functioning.

At this juncture of the argument it is not irrelevant to comment briefly upon the curiously modern, world-wide social phenomenon of juvenile delinquency that has made its appearance in such diverse settings as Norway, Japan, and Russia, no less than in England and America. Conceivably, this widespread situation indicates an intuitive perception and rejection of an adult world incommensurate with humanistic values—a world in which the individual as such is hopelessly isolated and superfluous. The adolescent, closer to instinctual adjustment than intelligent accord, is naturally more sensitive and uncompromising in his attitude towards this condition of universal alienation and negation than his elders and asserts himself accordingly in aimless and destructive revolt.

In speaking of the means of life we are principally concerned in our day with the world of the machine in its profuse ramifications, its endless inventions, its far-flung technological processes and procedures—the vast external apparatus of contemporary civilization. In speaking of the ultimate ends and aims of life, we are led, on the contrary, towards ever more distant goals that lie, undefined and intangible, on the far horizon of our visions. Patently, the dominant means of life are wholly unrelated to these ends and constitute a self-sufficient realm of their own. Having achieved a fair measure of security in the struggle for survival, we have learned, at least in the Western world, to spiral the means of life into an elaborate pursuit of surplus needs and original accomplishments—into ends, in short, that have the singular distinction of growing out of the means for achieving them. The very genesis of these ends endows them with an air of unreality, or at least of artificiality, which sets them apart from our ultimate ends and aims. Thus our dominant means and our ultimate goals are deeply separate, and the essential irrelevance of one to the other is revealed in all its decisive meaning by the fact that each sphere draws quite different aspects of the human psyche into play. If it is the province of man's spirit and intellect to be concerned with the far-off goals of life, it is the special province of intelligence, as we have seen, to administer and deal with the ever more intricate world of his means. But that world, in constituting the immensely elaborated foreground of life, has endowed intelligence with a unique and dominant role in modern life, for it is the task of intelligence to bind that world of immediate urgency into a functioning whole—a task which intelligence accomplishes by serving as the supreme means for the organization of all other means.

Intelligence, in thus structuring the manifold means of modern life, exercises an ever more sweeping and crucial function in sustaining the momentum of our civilization. That influence is apparent not only throughout the vast mesh of our explicit relationships, in all the tangible aspects of life, but in our encounters with the ever impinging challenges and contingencies of the future as well. Having achieved its most signal successes in the world of science and technology, in which the precise prediction of the future is the touchstone of validity, intelligence by a natural extension of its influence is increasingly called upon as a guiding principle of action in the less formulated realms of social existence. Here too, we may be certain, its impact will extend the element of predictability, ushering in a system of social relationships established on a basis of pragmatic and rational principles to supplant the prevailing confusion of obsolete conventions and sterile mores in a changing world. The trend is inevitable. But as the growing imbalance of modern life testifies, the swing of the pendulum is not without its own precarious consequences.

Looking at our predicament from the broad perspective of history, it is evident that we are striding boldly forward into what may prove a cul-de-sac of pure intelligence. In the course of our development, the influence of intelligence as a guiding principle of action and procedure has unmistakably followed an ascending curve, rising slowly even before the dawn of history and reaching a sharp crescendo with the advent of science, milleniums later. In the arena of human responses, some areas, it is clear, are more amenable to the operations of intelligence than others, while some indeed, like the problems of science and technology, lie almost wholly within the special province of intelligence. But it is noteworthy that the latter operations, challenges, or problems —however we define them—occupy an ever increasing measure of our conscious attention, and that, in the course of time, especially since the advent of scientific methodology, they have come to direct our actions and dominate our thinking. This situation has reached a climactic pitch for other reasons as well. In addition to the direct impress of science and technology, we are subtly transmuting the character of our problems and challenges by presenting them to ourselves in terms peculiarly suitable and inviting to the operations of intelligence. Thus both the questions and the answers are brought within the locus and domain of intelligence. Moreover, just as intelligence, once liberated from the adumbrating illusions and conceptions of the past, gave us the world of modern science, so, in turn, the pursuit of science revealed to us the potentialities of intelligence in a wholly new light. It may be said with some justice that, whereas man devoted himself throughout the ages to a rebirth and rejuvenation of his spiritual self, he succeeded instead to his own astonishment in coming upon the burgeoning of his intelligence in all its unsuspected power and sovereignty. And stumbling upon this profound disclosure, man has followed its light ever since. But this sweeping extension in the range and influence of intelligence was sustained, not so much in response to any deliberate policy or conscious insight, as to the inherent demands and compulsions of our ever more intricate civilization. In its unimpeded reach intelligence seems destined to enlarge the terrain of its sovereignty until it will have usurped the role of a supreme guiding principle in every aspect of life.

The operations of intelligence in the modern world have followed a twofold course. As we have noted, once the scientific conversion of the world became an established fact, the organizational impact of intelligence tended to shape the problems, dilemmas, and challenges of society in rational, scientific terms, that is to say, in terms appropriate and meaningful to a predominantly scientific milieu. Consciously as well as unconsciously, as a direct result of this trend the area of intuitive perceptions and emotional evaluations receded in favor of more precise, externalized, concrete formulations, until in time the panorama of life became fractured, as it were, into ever more predictable and workable fragments of itself. What the world lost in mystery and imagination, it gained in operational efficiency, in the functional organization and purposive orientation of its manifold aspects. Thus, not only are we impelled to set the problems and seek the answers to our social dilemmas in terms of intelligence, but we are equally determined to eliminate or transvalue all other psychic approaches in the task of overcoming our difficulties and meeting our challenges. In its pervasive drift, intelligence tends to encompass not only the world of science, in which its success has been complete, but that wholly scientific world which our civilization is rapidly approaching. And as a consequence of this sweeping rational predisposition, intelligence functions not merely as the dominant, but increasingly as the sole, principle of acceptable guidance in our affairs. We are challenged, accordingly, not with a critique of intelligence as such, functioning in its own right, but with intelligence, isolated and supreme, operating in a psychic vacuum, as it were, by itself. Such is the nature of the imbalance besetting us.

The problem of the future, seen in its larger aspects, is thus concerned above all with the crucial question of whether man has reached a point of no return—a phrase bearing a peculiarly modern connotation—in the fateful imbalance of his contemporary predicament.

III

Little is to be gained in attempting to answer this question by restricting ourselves to the harassment and confusion of our immediate perplexities. By all the standards of our historic past, we are moving into new terrain at an accelerating pace of totally unprecedented speed, into areas of totally unprecedented scope. Indeed, for the first time in human history we are conscious of a global, universal drift encompassing, in one fashion or another, the entire human race. This aspect of the problem alone is sufficient to indicate its profound depth and scope. In itself, however, it throws no light upon the meaning or direction of the vast transformation in which we find ourselves—a transformation that may well be described as a basic *change of phase* in the historic development of mankind as a whole.

In using the term "change of phase," I am appropriating a concept from the field of thermodynamics, in which it implies a change of form or structure, as, for example, occurs among three states of vapor, water, and ice. Whether this sense of the term applied to the historic process bears any analogy with its meaning in thermodynamics and the concept of entropy is a question first raised by Henry Adams early in the century and one which has remained virtually neglected and unanswered ever since. In an earlier book, *Posthistoric Man—An Inquiry*, I attempted to re-evaluate Adams' brilliant foray in somewhat different terms from those he used. Here an analogy was suggested between the machine—itself a perfect example of pure intelligence—and a crystal; under the conditions of our historic situation, the machine may be said to effect a basic change of phase in the structure of society through a sustained process of social crystallization or universal collectivization. The machine, accepted in its widest connotations, was pictured as the specific agency of a vast and essentially irreversible social transformation. For our present purposes the analogy, quite apart from the question of its ultimate validity, has the virtue of emphasizing the profoundly *structural* nature of the social changes we are entering upon, and it is mentioned here to stress again the crucial role of intelligence in bringing about an organizational transformation in the social life of mankind.

Leaning upon this analogy for the moment, we may rephrase the question concerning a point of no return in our imbalance. Is the organizational drift of the modern world the expression of a necessary and inescapable change of phase—a process of crystallization brought about by our machine technology under the dominant impact of human intelligence—or is it in all its massive scale an essentially flexible social phenomenon subject to our control and direction? Is the drift amenable to our wisdom and judgment in the achievement of a higher cultural, organic synthesis of life, or is it simply the expression of an inherent and irreversible trend in the historic development of mankind? Assuming that history, like evolution in general, represents an irreversible process, by what superior guidance may we hope to re-establish a balance we seem definitely to have lost? By what manner of psychic manipulation, of spiritual accommodation, of tangible, material adjustment, may we hope to realize the freedom necessary to accomplish this challenging task? Or shall we relax amidst the dark tension of the moment with the assurance that the trend of history will enter upon a new phase of human freedom if only we cease to "trouble about the happiness of individuals," in the words of Sigmund Freud? In short, to what extent and in what manner can we direct the universal drift towards increased organization and the concomitant collectivization of human society?

These questions have elicited many answers. The most sweeping response to the problem, however, is simply to deny its existence. Such is the accepted attitude if not the reasoned position of the world at large. The drift towards increased organization is seen not in its fateful totality but rather in terms of an axiomatic necessity in response to each specific challenge. Thus the fabric of society is silently transmuted. Immersed in the incidental procedures of this transformation, we are little inclined to question its social bearing or ultimate direction beyond extending the blessings of the system into the random and unpredictable areas of life that are still unclaimed by it. Today even the weather is no longer accepted in a spirit of resignation, and modern meteorology confidently anticipates the time when not only its predictions but the weather itself will be subject to precise control. Granting the likelihood of this enterprise, we can readily imagine the far-reaching organizational adjustments its realization would imply. Significantly, the elements of prediction and control—axiomatic in the fixed design of the machine—are becoming increasingly essential in every aspect of modern life; and this necessity may be directly equated with the insistent demand for increased organization throughout the length and breadth of our technologically oriented society. Viewed in this light, the expansion of organization appears not only inevitable, but necessary and desirable. The increased organization of life is seen as a goal rather than a problem, and any lingering doubts about its possible binding social effects, we are convinced, will "wither away" under the blissful conditions of ultimate freedom. The dilemma of our growing imbalance will be overcome by the ever more urgent expedient of "Newspeak," already in evidence in both China and Russia, where the impact of the problem is doubtless more apparent than in America. Here, we may expect to be no less ingenious in finding appropriate disguises, in the manner of Madison Avenue, as our own system of organization closes in upon us. Whether in time the Newspeak will evaporate as such, and future generations will accept their condition without a sense of regretful awareness and frustration, is another matter. Conditioned to an entirely new phase of human existence, they may well see their situation in another light, and the problem will have vanished, not because it will have been resolved, but because it will no longer be comprehended as such.

In a sense, this response to the situation, if not yet an actuality, is progressively becoming so. We are rapidly being conditioned by the converging forces of social conformity and social necessity as organization itself, spreading ever further afield, becomes at once more insistent and more subtle in its demands. The patent need for increased organization in a system already deeply organized permits no alternative and discourages critical dissent, while the incidental toll of its less conscious manifestations, though augmenting our prevailing imbalance, remains silently scattered and unacknowledged. Plainly, the aggressive expansion of organization throughout the social system has its own psychological repercussions. In the ensuing problems of social maladjustment, however, it is the individual rather than the social system that elicits attention, and here, needless to say, the overwhelming reality of the social factor dictates a wholly one-sided solution. It is the individual, in short, who must learn the lessons of conformity. At the same time, the psychologists and psychiatrists involved with problems of social maladjustment will find themselves subject to the same compulsion, and whether they recognize the situation with good grace or not, they too must accept the pervasive reality of the social structure as the datum line of their therapy. It is true that members of the psychologic fraternity, beginning with Sigmund Freud himself, have increasingly recognized the need for a therapeutic approach to the ills of society as a whole, but thus far their efforts and their theories in this domain have remained singularly barren and unproductive. However valid theoretically, this approach to the problem has its own inherent difficulties, not the least of which is the fact that probably most practitioners in the field are themselves adequately adjusted conformists for whom a basic reversal in the structure of their social values would involve little short of a psychic somersault. The difficulty is similar to an equally grave dilemma in the field of education: the age-old question of how and by whom the teacher is to be educated in the first place. In the psychologic field, as elsewhere in the organized milieu of modern society, adjustment to the social system is a primary and mandatory requirement binding upon each of the individuals composing it. But the means by which this requirement is accomplished in our society grow increasingly compulsory, external, and impersonal, and unlike the inherited and more stable mores of primitive society, they leave a residue of psychic disorders and maladjustments in their wake. This situation, however, is clearly a transitional phenomenon, testifying to the speed of our changing milieu; in time, as the system approaches stability and equilibrium, its internal frictions are certain to subside and eventually to vanish. The nightmarish techniques of *1984*, plausibly suggested by the practices of today, will be supplanted, we may be sure, by rationalized, far-reaching psychic and ideologic modes of indoctrination, if only because they will prove superior in achieving without tension what the former methods were intended to achieve through fear and horror. Even the notion of dictatorship, however interpreted, may in time be superseded by more balanced, secure, and enduring scientific methods of social control and procedure.

The widely accepted response to the problems and difficulties of increased organization, which consists primarily in denying their validity by throwing the onus of doubt and suspicion upon the individual rather than upon the prevailing trends of society, must itself be counted a sign that we may well have passed a point of no return in the ominous spiral of organization. Social conformity, however arbitrarily contrived or consciously accepted, is looked upon as an axiomatic mandate of modern society, and perhaps no aspect of our dilemma is more revealing in this respect than the fact, previously commented upon, that oppositional movements to the trend of events must themselves conform, at least to the extent of being organized, in order to achieve mere survival. Failing that, such movements dissolve into scattered groups of disparate individuals exercising neither influence nor authority, while the drift of organization advances unabated, like an onrushing train, leaving the litter of the roadbed behind in a flurry of futile protest. Conscientious objectors to war, for example, whose opposition to a collective movement of society is based presumably upon a sacred prerogative of the individual, found it expedient to organize in order to establish their position more firmly. This paradoxical action is symptomatic of the fate of individualism, whatever its form, in our society: either the individuals harboring a common purpose or sharing a common attitude must organize or their efforts are doomed to evaporate into meaningless gestures of futile and isolated protest.

Obviously, no frontal attack upon the problem will avail to reduce the incidence of organization in modern life or to mitigate its rising momentum in the direction of a condition of complete and universal domination. Intelligence here speaks a language of unequivocal aims, while life under our technological demands becomes necessarily impervious to other voices. Having established the pattern of our social mode of operation, we can tolerate no alternatives; and the inherent necessity of organization becomes thereby ever more final and unarguable. Organization in the social realm leads to the same uncompromising perfection demanded in the design and operation of the machine.

None the less, in assessing the meaning and direction of our organizational drift it would be cavalier in the extreme to brush aside the deeply rooted countervailing influences of our cultural heritage. Indeed, it is precisely their sustained power in the bloodstream of our ideas that accounts for the psychic and spiritual dislocations of modern life: it is the tension and pressure of these influences that have left us with an imbalance in our society and a crisis in our culture. The entire tradition of humanist values, based upon the spiritual primacy of the self, is now at stake. Nor is this surprising: in a social no less than a physical change of phase, we are confronted by a transformation of universal scope, and the ensuing disorientation in our sense of values will continue to reveal itself, we may be sure, in endless and astonishing aspects. As we have noted earlier, not the least meaningful among these in its social bearing is the startling acceptance accorded to modern art, whose sensational explorations—which in other times might well have passed as travesties—now gain an oblique significance against the backdrop of modern life. Here, whether in music or literature, poetry or choreography, painting or sculpture, with their common emphasis upon the intangible, hidden, unconscious responses of mind and soul, we must recognize the affirmation of an elemental sensibility, a forgotten meaning, lost in the ultrarational milieu of our technological civilization. How else are we to interpret the willfully obscure, enigmatic, nonobjective character of this symbolic art except as a search for the intuitive, spontaneous voices of our buried selves? Its inscrutability is a transparent avowal of the irrational—a countervailing gesture of opposition in an otherwise rationalized, mechanized, truncated environment—and it is not surprising that modern art has accordingly been rejected and condemned by the protective authority of totalitarian regimes, whether of the right or of the left. Its anarchic sources of power betray a secret threat; hence it has been systematically disowned as puerile, decadent, antisocial. Actually, its arrows of protest are often shot into the dark; with its hidden meaning and abstruse symbolism, it has an often poignant and melancholy air. With a few exceptions, it remains a defensive affirmation, a deeply personal and fragmented protest against the bland rationality and impervious surfaces of modern existence. In its totality, it must be accepted as an anguished expression of bewilderment in a world that is undergoing a fateful and sweeping inversion of the very sources of its values.

Perhaps the visual arts, in particular, have been forced to an extremity of expression, though the modern novel, with its darkly turgid stream of language, and modern poetry, with its elegant incomprehensibility, are not far behind. Nor may we omit modern music, with its emphasis upon shrill atonality and sharp dissonances. Modern art reflects a fractured universe. If contemporary art is born out of a ruptured world, the social philosophers of the day have at least attempted to take the measure of that discord in more critically cogent and precisely articulated terms. Yet their findings are not readily summarized—partly because they represent divergent aspects of the scene, but mainly, perhaps, because we have only just entered upon the transformation they would assess. We are looking for a new vocabulary of ideas and ideals, for a new relation between individual and society, for a new humanism, a new religion, a new and more searching comprehension of science, and above all for a new and embracing synthesis of life in all its manifold and bewildering aspects. We are living in a febrile age of mounting problems, in which hope and despair alternate in an anguished dance, for we are lost in a turmoil of values at the very moment when we would establish their immutable foundations or acknowledge in desperation their final relativity. Meanwhile, we are silently foundering amidst the aims and ends of life, while devoting our critical intelligence as never before to the perfection of our means. And beneath the assured progress of our technology, we find ourselves none the less anxious and perplexed, as though the promised future might after all turn out to be a mirage in a dissolving world.

All of this is merely to reiterate what has been said before—that we are at a crossroad in our affairs. To the robust and discerning minds of the age, this situation constitutes a challenge to establish a new *Weltanschauung*, a creative synthesis commensurate with the potentialities of the modern world. But however diverse in approach, a common dilemma haunts these efforts. Seen from one aspect, the world is subject to an overriding principle of universal organization—a vast converging movement towards an ever more integrated world. Seen from another angle, the world appears to be undergoing a profound fragmentation, a dissolution and disintegration of our inwardly established spectrum of values. Basically, we are at one in attempting to reconcile these divergent aspects of contemporary life; our critical differences arise in the varied approaches we pursue to achieve a principle of "convergent integration," in the words of Julian Huxley. Our approaches to the future, however, are rooted perforce in our responses to the past; and the dilemma confronting us, we are beginning to suspect, may continue to trouble us in the future as it has in the past, if only because it arises out of the very texture of the human mind, rather than the prevailing conditions of our environment.

IV

In tracing the evolution of mankind through its various stages or transformations, we become aware of a persistent counterpoint in its development. In particular, throughout the relatively short period of his historic development, man has been subject to a polarity rooted, on the one hand, in his spiritual nature, which has found expression in his varied religions, and on the other hand, in his rational intelligence, which, perhaps more than any other factor, molded the gradually coalescing forms of his diverse civilizations. But man, seeking always a harmonious synthesis between the inwardly and outwardly directed components of his psyche, having passed through a series of changing cultures in his search for unity, is now confronted in the age of science by a more crucial and decisive challenge than ever before. The drama of this challenge is heightened, moreover, by the fact that for the first time humanity seems in sight of attaining, in balanced and creative form, a new "world culture" of unpredictable potential.

The transformations of man are tokens of a continuous emergence, and the history of mankind, despite its shadowed aspects, is the story of a struggle towards an ideal of increasing perfection and transcendence. However much man may have wavered in his response to the polarities of his nature, he has in general carried forward the heritage of the past, while enlarging his experience, his knowledge, and his insight sufficiently to reshape that heritage into a continuous preparation towards a richer and more abundant future. Today, however, secure in his scientific attainments, modern man seems content to forgo the search for that higher synthesis he has never yet attained to the fullness of his hopes or has attained at best only in the example of the rarest individuals. As a consequence of this tangential approach to the meaning of existence, he now finds himself increasingly adrift, an isolated and fragmented being, submerged within the set forms of an ever more rigid social collectivity in lieu of his position as an individual, a person, in a viable community of persons. Under these circumstances, how is man to overcome this threatening imbalance, which is steadily undermining his status as the influences of group psychology and totalitarian domination converge to dilute and at length eliminate his personality?

In a sense the question answers itself. We must restore the concept of the person to a position of fructifying centrality and must make the community once again a free plenum of creative individuals. However elaborated, this is the essential thesis of humanism. And however maintained—whether from a basically philosophic or religious approach, from a sociologic or psychologic or ethical angle—this position emphasizes the primacy of the individual as the fountainhead and source of human consciousness and human values. Moreover, only as values are absorbed and echoed within the individual soul will they possess the quality of a living force, a dynamic and creative potency beyond and above the residue of inert creeds and socially conventional doctrines. "Man's principal task today," writes Lewis Mumford in *The Transformations of Man*, "is to create a new self, adequate to command the forces that operate so aimlessly and yet so compulsively." Perhaps no one concerned with the challenge of the future has been more aware of the profound disturbances of the contemporary scene, while sustaining at the same time a faith in the ultimate fulfillment of human potentialities, than Lewis Mumford. The depth of his humanism and the wealth of knowledge and insight that supports it merit our special attention. Aware that the world is moving towards a dismal unification on the basis of its technological demands alone, Mr. Mumford, fully aware, too, that such an eventuality will invite a universal totalitarianism, goes on to observe, "The very possibility of achieving a world order by other means than totalitarian enslavement and automation rests on the plentiful creation of unified personalities, at home with every part of themselves, and so equally at home with the whole family of man, in all its magnificent diversity. Unified man must accept the id without giving it primacy: he must foster the superego, without making it depress the energies it needs for its own fuller expression. Without fostering such self-knowledge, balance, and creativity, a world culture might easily become a compulsive nightmare." And in the same place, emphasizing the need of a new self in response to the demands of a new world order, he writes, "In short, world civilization will have its own tensions, difficulties, even perils, peculiar to itself; and the solution of these problems will call for political imagination of the highest order. Many of its problems will prove insurmountable, indeed, until the same needs that have produced the beginnings of these institutions bring forth, in the fullness of time, a higher order of personality, capable of perfecting them. Both the agent and the goal of this transformation is unified man."

The possibility of attaining a higher world culture is thus seen to be contingent upon the presence of what might be termed world personalities—men of supreme capacities, devoted to the enhancement of human potentialities and the widening of human perspectives, whose influence would sustain lesser men in the common task of creating a new world. Mankind has known such personalities: in the age of the "axial religions" men were profoundly influenced by Buddha, by Confucius, by Moses, by Ikhnaton in his short-lived reign, as later they were influenced by Jesus and Mohammed. If today we seem to lack men of their stamp, it is owing in part to the vast expansion and greater complexity of the modern world, but more perhaps to the paradoxical fact that we have recourse to world-wide and instantaneous communication—a condition that reduces to human proportions the most inspired redeemer. Indeed, in our age, it will be granted, the evil influence of Adolf Hitler was as pervasive as and far more effective than the good influence of Mahatma Gandhi, whose philosophy of life is even now being reluctantly abandoned by his followers. But more significantly, we seem consigned in our predicament to cultivating the growth of personalities at a moment when the very soil of our culture is being systematically leached of every nutrient element; we are left, as it were, to build the house of the future with materials that are vanishing before our eyes. The eventual eclipse of the individual, following upon the impoverishment of his personality, constitutes the essence of the problem confronting us: how may we hope to reverse a trend that grows more ominous and implacable as the individual, lost in the collectives of the future, disappears from the scene?

Mindful of the threatening constrictions which the drift of modern life imposes upon us, Lewis Mumford maintains an attitude of courageous hope on the basis of Clerk Maxwell's principle of "singular points." The full quotation covering this point is given below from Mumford's *The Conduct of Life*.

Maxwell's doctrine gives exactly the insight needed into the present situation. He pointed out that even in the simplest physical systems at rare intervals there are moments which he called singular points. At these points an infinitely small force through its character and position in the whole constellation of events, is able to bring about a change of almost unbelievable magnitude, as with a pebble starting a landslide. This doctrine allows for the impact of human personality in history, not only by mass movements, but by individuals and small groups who are sufficiently alert to intervene at the right time and the right place for the right purpose. At such moments—do they not obviously account for Gautama, Jesus, Mohammed?—a single human personality may overcome the apparently irresistible inertia of institutions. Happily, as Maxwell pointed out, the higher and more complex the system, the more often do singular points occur in it: there are more singular points in the biologic system than in the physical system, more in man's life than in an ant's. So our sense of what is now possible is not in fact sound unless it makes allowance for what, on the basis of the known, the typical, the predictable, would be an extravagant impossibility.

Acknowledging the waywardness of singular points, Mumford himself refers to them as "miracles." It is to be observed,

CHALLENGE OF INTELLIGENCE

however, that even singular points require a favorable concatenation of events: the pebble causing an avalanche requires an accommodating slope and the prophet whose impress will move humanity will have to arise at a propitious moment in a milieu favorable to his mission. Moreover, the doctrine of Maxwell applied to human affairs fails to distinguish between good and evil; it allows for a Napoleon or a Stalin—not to mention a Hitler—no less than for a Gandhi. Even so, we must take into account, on a deeper plane, the direction of our scientifically oriented technological civilization. We are moving, inherently, towards a state of ever greater *predictability* in the functioning of our affairs—a principle, we may recall, based on the implicit operation of intelligence in furthering the organization of our increasingly involved and complex technological world. In the turmoil of our transformation, while the values and ideals of the past still exert a countervailing influence, we may indeed find ourselves in a more or less hectic state of change. But we are certain to experience a steady diminution in the vagaries of life, in its capriciousness and uncertainty, as we enter the increasingly planned society of the future. Such, clearly, is the overwhelming drift of events. Whether the vanishing interstices of life will allow future miracles becomes thereby increasingly dubious; and our predicament takes on the appearance of a desperate hope, sustained by the memory of rare examples from a past we are rapidly leaving behind us. Reluctantly, we are thus forced to abandon Lewis Mumford's approach to the future as a grave but disheartening appraisal, or at best, with all due allowances, as a tangential hope based upon a faith that the miracles of the future will not only sprout in the soil of a planned society, but that they will surpass in their overwhelming power the miracles of the past, which have thus far failed to prevent our present impasse.

It is all too apparent that the historic "miracles" of the past have not prevented the world of mankind from falling into its present dilemma. In a sense, this may well be interpreted to mean that even the wisest of men have failed to encompass the future. Or again, with perhaps equal validity it may be said that humanity has consistently bypassed the wisdom and insight available to it. So long as we maintain our faith in the continued occurrence and efficacy of singular points, however, we need have no fear of reaching a point of no return. Obviously there is no such crucial moment in the *Weltanschauung* of Lewis Mumford; hence his often hortatory tone, his dedication and inspiration. On the other hand, in his ardent search for the wholeness of man, on which alone we may hope to build the higher synthesis of a viable world culture, he has stopped short of entertaining a mystical faith in man's ultimate triumph. Thus, after all, a note of urgency pervades his message. But this final hesitation in the sources of his attitude constitutes in fact a kind of metaphysical hiatus that weakens rather than strengthens a philosophic position based ultimately upon humanistic principles alone.

In contrast, the mystical approach of Waldo Frank, whose intuitive acumen and metaphysical awareness carry him beyond the purely cultural synthesis of Mumford into a search for a newly articulated relationship to God, expressive of the fullness of man's nature, in his essentially religious approach to the destiny of mankind voices a perhaps more remote but more profound summation of our dilemma. Here the rays of our spiritual aspirations are seen to culminate in the concept of God; and conversely, only in the concept of God can the brotherhood of man come to full and adequate realization. The "singular points" which Mumford hopefully looks forward to in the womb of the future, Frank conceives of as lying in the life of each individual—the moments of mystical illumination that would convert individuals into persons, members of the brotherhood of man and the fellowship of God. Waldo Frank believes this illumination to be the fruit of spiritual self-discipline; in consequence, he is inclined to be didactic where Mumford is hortatory. But like Mumford, and indeed like most of our humanist and religious philosophers, his approach to the solution of our difficulties begins with the transformation of the individual, extending through small groups of individuals to effective units of ever larger groups. And though his approach is metaphysically more deeply rooted, it too founders, in the face of our increasingly organized, outwardly directed civilization, in being based upon the tenuous faith that the shrinking spiritual oases left to man will in time spread to encompass the world. Yet in his book *The Rediscovery of Man*, Frank is keenly aware of the enormity and centrality of this very problem, of how the *organic* deteriorates into the *organizational* as it spreads from its source in the person to ever more ambiguous and equivocal groups. "... the maturation of the human world," he writes there, "can never begin, unless the groups by which the world works and lives mature.... The historic problem is still before us. But to approach it we have these immediate bridgeheads...." And here we are again presented a vision of mature persons, creatively "subversive" groups, few and scattered though they may be, controverting the dominant trends and inherent drift of our civilization by the intensity of their spiritual vision and spiritual energy. "Quantitative psychological change in a group," he continues, "*can* become qualitative: at what point of saturation, who can say?" Unfortunately, this observation is true quite apart from the intrinsic value of the psychologic change; indeed, it is far truer in accounting for the psychologically deadening effects of organized procedures in our ever more highly organized society than it is in sustaining, in reverse, the organic, spiritual influences of isolated personalities. Theoretically, no doubt, it might be maintained that we function along a two-way street, as it were; actually, the overwhelming procedural direction of modern civilization must be accepted for what it is—a one-way thoroughfare. Thus the underlying hope expressed in Waldo Frank's observation, buttressed though it is by a mystical faith, is none the less akin to Lewis Mumford's faith and hope in singular points. Hope does, indeed, tell us in which direction we are facing; it does not tell towards which direction we are moving.

Finally, we must come to terms with the mystical basis of Waldo Frank's philosophy—not perhaps in respect to its validity in the spiritual transformation of the individual, but to the specific problem before us: the spiritual transformation of society. True, this is necessarily to come about through the activation of individuals, but therein lies, as we have repeatedly noted, the deep crux of the problem. Clearly, as the pressure of the problem increases, its solution recedes. But perhaps it will be argued that man, pursuing his inevitable orbit, will reach, not a point of no return, but a breaking point: thereupon he will at length be freed from his self-imposed shackles and in the depths of his being find himself in God and God in his self. Man will have completed the cycle of his imbalance and returned, on a higher and more profound level, to the challenge he first encountered in the time of his axial religions. A new dawn will come in the revelation of man's relation to the cosmos and to God. Such, briefly, is the mystic vision of his ultimate redemption.

Now, it must be confessed that faith is a dimension beyond all argument; and the sober probabilities of the future recede before its nameless potentialities—indeed, one might almost have said with equal force, before its miraculous improbabilities. Yet a teleological intuition has haunted the mind of man from the beginning, reshaping his finite world in infinite terms. Traditionally, the mystics, whether of the Orient or the Occident, have expressed this vision in the language of paradox. This curious resort to paradox proceeds not from a perverse intransigence, but arises in response to the need of establishing a metaphysical bridge in human terms between the finite world of the senses and the equally real but infinite world beyond. Paradox is the natural language of transcendence: it serves as a ladder without rungs leading from the visible to the invisible. It occurs, incidentally, as Cassius J. Keyser pointed out long ago, in the domain of mathematics, whose truths might well serve as proper symbols for the vision of the mystics. Thus, for example, we learn that the number of points in any arc of a circle is equal to the number of points in the circle itself: the part is equal to the whole. Therewith the empirical system of concrete fact dissolves before our eyes and we are adrift in a world at once finite and infinite. How is man to come to terms with himself and his universe, caught in this insolvable predicament? If he has never yet found a satisfactory answer, the mystics among men have at least stated the problem and suffered its unending challenge. And from the residue of futile speculation they have salvaged an inner truth, for by the depth of their awareness they alone live in both realms. Not until mankind as a whole achieves a like intensity of consciousness, however, can we speak of its spiritual transcendence; and though, in the realm of logic, this improbability still remains a possibility, we are clearly moving in a contrary direction under the aegis of our reigning intelligence. Here a profound distinction between wisdom and intelligence sobers our anticipations—between that wisdom which arises in the illumined soul of the mystic and the socially nurtured intelligence of mankind in general. We live in a pragmatically truncated world, the world of increasingly ordered intelligence rather than the spontaneous world of mystic wisdom. And even though we envisage in the dim future the actual breakdown of a system and condition of life built upon the former, we are merely desperately hopeful in seeing this collapse as the dark night of rebirth instead of as a final world catastrophe or, at the least, as a calamitous relapse into savagery. Nor may we hope to rise from such a condition to anything like our present status, if only because, as Harrison Brown has shown in his perceptive analysis, the readily available natural resources of the earth will long since have been exhausted. The course of history, however, is not prone to reverse itself, as though human destiny shuttled back and forth within the confines of a limited repertory. If human history is unlikely to reverse itself, the human species, like other species, may none the less have in store for it a period of incredible stability, ending, perhaps, in a harmony with the larger aspects of evolutionary development, in a final eclipse due precisely to the fateful specialization of its cerebral development. The darkness of that night will not be followed by the dawn of a rebirth.

However we arrange the factors of our impending destiny, however we view, whether with hope or doubt, the perspective of the future, we are deeply aware of a race with time. We live, by common consent, in a crucial epoch of history, in a period of climactic significance. This sense of time, of climax, substantiates the intuitive perception of a point of no return in the trajectory of our present course. Yet, what can we mean by such a phrase in view of the fact that history, like evolution in general, is an irreversible process consisting, after all, of nothing but "points of no return"? Clearly, we can only mean that we are coming to a parting of the ways, to the ridge of a watershed, in the course of our long historic development. Whatever the nature of this transformation, we may be certain that in scope and depth it will reach to the roots of our being. Yet, by all the signs of the time, it will not encompass a *transfiguration* of man. On the contrary, if we accept the universal drift towards increased organization in modern life as the sign of our inescapable homage to intelligence, we must see in the resulting "massification" and collectivization of mankind a ruthless depersonalization of man. The transcendence of man into a cosmic-centered being—the person as defined by Waldo Frank in his book *The Rediscovery of Man*—is thus seen to lie in an opposite direction from our universal drift. Astute and realistic in his criticism of our civilization, Frank freely acknowledges this point. "Man with his present ego image of self and collective self," he writes there, "certainly cannot cope with the mounting pathology of a mechanized order which, paradoxically, as it swarms because of a lowered death rate, as it increases comfort and multiplies leisure, threatens man at his heart." And, as though in answer to his own decimating judgment upon contemporary man, he looks to the future, however distant, with a faith based upon a wholly mystic eschatology. "Man's power over nature," he says in a later passage of this seminal book, "would have seemed impossible to the science of a century ago. Man's methodic search for the reality of selfhood by which alone disaster can be transmuted into life seems impossible to the common ethic and psychology of our day. A shrewd impossibilism must be the standard of every fighter in this battle. The dimension that must be known is the dimension of depth. In this sense, every volunteer finds himself aloof from the periphery of human intercourse—hidden—a dweller in catacombs. How long he remains there with his fellows, how long before the catacombs become the streets of a new city under the sun, no one may say." The "shrewd impossibilism" of this position is but an acknowledgement of a deep and stubborn dilemma; and the burden of these quotations, taken side by side, would seem to narrow the hope of escape from this dilemma to the mystical vision of an inner cosmos.

V

In the "transhumanism" of Julian Huxley, on the other hand, we are assured that mankind may transcend itself "not just sporadically, an individual here in one way, an individual there in another, but in its entirety, as humanity," provided only that humanity will accept the task which evolution has at length placed within its powers. In his "Evolutionary Humanism," however,

Julian Huxley recognizes certain complexities. "There is inevitably," he writes further, "some conflict between the interests of individuals and those of society. But the conflict is in large measure transcended in this conception of man as an evolving psycho-social organism. This dictates certain conclusions. In the longest point of view, our aim must be to develop a type of society and culture capable of ever-fresh evolution, one which continually opens the way to new and fuller realizations: in the medium point of view, we must secure the reproduction and improvement of psycho-social organization, the maintenance of the frame-works of society and culture and their transmission and adjustment in time; and in the immediate point of view we must aim at maximum individual fulfillment." Alas! the keystone of this far-flung structure is missing at the very moment when we would begin its erection: once again we must seek to attain the wholeness of the individual when his very identity is being threatened as never before, while we are left with few or no hints about how we may reverse the course of events and stop our advance long enough to change its direction.

Nor may we find any more comfort in such a book as Erich Kahler's *The Tower and the Abyss,* in which the "oasis" solution of the problem reminds us in our ubiquitous spiritual impoverishment of the catacombs of Waldo Frank. The search for "communality" in place of "collectivity" is but another approach to the same problem—the elimination of the individual, as such, in the society of the future. Erich Kahler is aware of the historic transformation of the individual. "All the symptoms which we have observed," he remarks, "indicate that we are in a state of transition from the individual to a broader, supra-individual form of existence." At the same time, "The experience of an inner, human community fades away under the pressure of collectives... which are purely external, mechanical groupings for partial and functional purposes, partial not only in the sense of specialization, but also inasmuch as they tend to stifle the inner, human part of the human being. A collective will never be able to restore meaning to human life; it will never afford a true control of man over his world grown out of bounds."

The subtitle of Erich Kahler's book is *An Inquiry into the Transformation of the Individual*, but a reading of the book, which has a sharp insight into the nature of our dilemma, does little to sustain the wistful hope of converting our descent into the abyss into an ascent towards the tower. Basically, this hope springs from the concept of man as a creature who will carry over into the forms of the future the highest values of his essential humanity. To accomplish this, however, the prevailing drift towards collectivity must be reversed in the teeth of a process that is everywhere subverting the individual and the humanism that sustains his significance. If primitive man achieved a "communality" that effectively held the individual within its orbit, modern man finds himself uprooted in all but the arbitrary, external bonds of his organizational commitments; as a result, he is no longer a fit vessel for the spiritual cargo he is supposedly carrying over into the communality of the future. But how, then, is the continuity of our cultural, humanistic tradition to be maintained? Patently the question is more easily asked than answered. The dominant aim of modern life may perhaps be summarized as the attainment of an ever more efficient and above all predictable security; in this milieu, however, the character of life takes on the character of an effective sieve, draining away the bothersome dross of spontaneous creativity and spiritual freedom. Thus life is being systematically bleached of its inner values, and an entirely new conformation of society, as Erich Kahler himself predicts, is destined to replace the society we know. The structural changes implicit in this transformation will constitute a true metamorphosis of the social conditions of mankind, in which the individual as such will disappear. We seem indeed to have little choice but to accept the irrefutable implications of this change. Not the human being in all his multi-dimensional potentialities, not the free-ranging individual, but a carefully regimented and deliberately adjusted mass of mankind will float in unison towards the shores of the future.

A sharp inversion of this presentiment is to be found in the unitary philosophy of Lancelot Law Whyte. The unison spoken of above is the direct consequence of the extrusion of the individual from the social mass of man; according to the unitary interpretation of Whyte as outlined in his book, *The Next Development in Man*, the grave dualism between individual and society is but one aspect of the general dissociation of Western civilization, aggravated during the last two thousand years, but destined to disappear as we enter upon a fundamental transformation now in the making. Under the impact of this unitary transformation, the individual will not be negated, but rather absorbed and integrated into the social fabric of the future as "one of the many formative organs of the social process." For a new and more comprehensive interpretation of life will have established a harmonious integration—a unity in diversity—releasing us at long last from the sterile paradoxes and misleading dualities of the past.

Whyte's philosophy is particularly pertinent precisely because he recognizes a basic dissociation beneath our civilization—a dissociation that he believes has now run its course and exhausted itself. Thus he foresees a pivotal shift in the spectrum of our values, carrying us from our former anchorage in a false dualism of change in a world of static forms and concepts to a new interpretation of life and nature as essentially processes in development. "In life development is primary and permanence secondary," he writes in the volume mentioned, "but in the history of thought permanence has to be understood before development. From this paradox arises the metaphysical confusion and spiritual tragedy of intellectual man." And more generally, not until man has transcended this paradox can he recover his erstwhile unity of spirit and thereby escape from the perplexing dualities of his inherited traditions of thought and action. Whyte believes that in human history, as in biologic development, dualism and conflict are always superimposed on a prior unity. This unity may be recovered, however, by healing the dissociation arising out of the long-sustained conflict between reason and instinct that has characterized European civilization. The lack of any clear co-ordinating tendencies in the meaning of our lives, the limitations at the base of our quantitative sciences, and the awkward disintegration of our values, are but the signposts of a strategic impasse in this conflict. And at this juncture in our affairs only a unitary science, indeed only a comprehensive unitary approach to life in all its aspects, can restore the integrative unity of man.

Persuasive as the argument appears, it is sometimes marred and even confused by the fact that the elucidation of the meaning of a unitary philosophy is often couched in the very terms to be illuminated. Consequently, one seems at times to be following a vast tautology made intelligible only in profile references to its essential meaning. It is apparent, however, that the two-thousand-year detour of Western man which has deposited him in his present impasse is rooted in a far more profound dichotomy in the human psyche than Whyte is prepared to grant. The "war" between reason and instinct may well have been superimposed upon a prior unity in the biologic condition of primitive man, but it was precisely this schism in his psychic nature that gave birth to his civilizations. Moreover, it was the cumulative nature of knowledge—especially in the case of European man—that augmented his dilemma. Conceivably human knowledge, as we have indicated, may reach a limiting condition and turn into a perimeter of the future at some remote date, but long before we have attained this precondition of a unitary balance and harmony between instinct and reason, we will have become encased in a static formulation of life processes. The conclusion seems inevitable: the dichotomous structure of man's psychic being is too deeply rooted to be bridged by a belated realization of its nature. In a postscript to his book, Whyte himself declares, "Unitary man is an organizer, he sets out to order his finite world." But the organizational approach to the problem is in itself the very core of the problem; and the dilemma into which we have sunk will not be resolved by a higher synthesis of human potentialities so much as by a drastic and final reliance upon reason in place of instinct as the decisive principle of guidance in our future conduct. In speaking of the "finite world" of unitary man—a world capable of being organized—we have unwittingly acknowledged a limitation not only in the case of unitary man but of modern man in general. The conception of unitary man sheds light upon our predicament; it does little to resolve it.

Nor is it plausible to believe, in view of all the lamentable testimony of the past, that the countervailing influences of contemporary life will succeed in developing the strength, stamina, and spiritual consecration necessary to become truly and effectively dominant. Neither the futile cultivation of Zen Buddhism among scattered circles of Western intellectuals, nor the sense of the "absurd" in the brave revolt of a Camus, nor yet the vast residue of human irrationality itself, is likely to restore us to a more balanced way of life or a sober realization of our predicament. The forces that carry us onward today, though they burst forth with bewildering power and finality only during the last few centuries, represent nothing less than the climactic dominance of intelligence in the complex orchestration of our psychic potentialities. This is the paradoxical kernel of our situation—a situation that leaves us uprooted and adrift, subject only to the coercion of socially oriented values under the effective sway of organizational patterns of thought and feeling, movement and action.

VI

Conceivably, human consciousness stems from the tension, peculiar to man, between instincts and intelligence. In the case of man alone has intelligence, clarified and emancipated by his unique faculty of speech, challenged the primordial sway of the instincts. This twofold approach in the struggle for existence doubtless insured man's triumphant position in the biologic hierarchy; and beyond that, in the growing intensity of his awareness, it endowed man with the extraordinary and explicitly human capacity of attaining a cumulative culture. Thus arose the towering edifices of his varied civilizations. It seems clear, moreover, in view of the ever changing aspects of man's development and the accelerating tempo in which these changes occurred, that the relationship between his instincts and his intelligence has been anything but static. In the course of time, on the contrary, the unresolved tension between them has taken on the character of a conflict, accompanied by a deepening of man's consciousness and a rising crescendo of change in his affairs. Patently, it is the influence of intelligence, struggling against the ingrained stability of the instincts, which is the moving factor in this panorama of change; and we are thus impelled to ask what the nature of its trajectory is—towards what goal, towards what end and aim is intelligence destined to carry us?

The question is in large measure obscured by the very duality of our psychic equipment. That is perhaps why man has been inspired since the days of the early Greeks, and doubtless far earlier, by an ideal of balance, of the harmonious union of his multiple faculties, of attaining, in brief, an ever higher synthesis of his psychic forces. Today possibly even more than in antiquity, we speak of the wholeness of the personality as the signature of psychic health and maturity. Yet, the rareness of its occurence, the pain, frustration, uncertainty, and strain that are the common lot of modern man, the imbalance of his society, and the lack of spiritual orientation in his affairs, lead us to ask whether that ideality is not perhaps based upon a questionable hope inherited from a less complex past, from a time at once more stable and more limited than the world of our day. We have subscribed, all too readily it would seem, to the notion that man is naturally capable of achieving a dynamic equilibrium that will carry him from one synthesis to an ever higher synthesis in the progressive realization of his latent potentialities. Having long since turned our backs upon Jean Jacques Rousseau's dream of an idyllic past, we are now anticipating a paradise of the future in the full splendor of our attainments. But if we have long smiled at Rousseau's fantasy, we are beginning to have doubts about our own and with a growing uneasiness are wondering whether the fundamental compatibility of our psychic make-up is not after all an illusion. Thus far, it is clear, history has given us little reason to believe our faith is based upon anything more than a convenient assumption which is becoming more difficult to maintain as the imbalance of our own technological civilization becomes ever more decisive and alarming.

In the blaze of our unexpected achievements, however, we are inclined to let the question go by default. If intelligence, in its latter-day triumphs, appears to have set a tangential course for mankind, we seem content to accept it as a provisional detour, to be corrected in due time, or again, in our growing alienation from the past, as the highroad to the brave new world of the future. But in any event, however we interpret the ever more preponderant influence of intelligence in our affairs, the point of greatest significance for us is the basic inevitability of our situation. Clearly, we can neither modify nor deflect the impact of intelligence, even if we would, by any agency other than a spiritual transfiguration of mankind in which intelligence itself is at length transcended by an aloof, profound, and encompassing wisdom. And though such a vista of the future cannot be rejected as altogether improbable, it must reluctantly be set aside as wholly visionary in view of the inherent restrictions to it we have already discussed. Apart from the over-all direction of our civilization, we are confronted today by three problems of supreme significance—the threat of atomic war, overpopulation, and the rapid exhaustion of our natural resources, not to mention the disastrous poverty in which three-quarters of the world still languishes. In view of their importance, indeed their ominous reality, we must grant that our efforts to solve these pressing and overt problems have thus far remained tragically inadequate, if they have not been altogether frustrated. How much more inaccessible and remote must we hold the prospects of a spiritual transfiguration of all mankind? On the other hand, our approach to the specific problems mentioned above will patently involve a deepening of our organizational trends and procedures—a further implementation of our socially oriented intelligence. But in this respect the problems are merely typical of our age, for today no problem is susceptible of solution apart from its congruity with the organizational structure of society in general. Even the dilemmas and difficulties of modern life that may be ascribed to human frailty, to the cupidity and selfish passions of men, are approached not as spiritual challenges so much as legal, or economic, or political problems, subject to the regulatory influence of organized intelligence. But the same attitudes and procedures operate with even greater finality in respect to the larger problems of world affairs. Let us take as an example one of the gravest challenges confronting mankind: war. Conceivably this profoundly tragic and ingrained evil will at last be eliminated because we have here reached a special perimeter of the future—total annihilation! Fear will have accomplished what all the spiritual affirmations throughout the ages failed to accomplish. And though the world is saved, humanity will have failed. The lesson has its obvious corollaries. While beneath the outward mechanisms of social planning and control we may indeed achieve a more efficient and effective confrontation of life and the world, we will at the same time have augmented the organizational pattern of society, with its inevitable externalization of values and concomitant structural crystallization of life. The basic problems of the age, which in a deep and profound sense have been evoked by intelligence, will have to be resolved by intelligence despite its inherent limitations. For we have entered, unawares, a cul-de-sac from which there appears to be, for us, no other escape. If intelligence has been a mounting factor throughout the varied phases of our long evolution, it promises to dominate in ever fuller measure our destiny in the future.

That is not to say the future will be free of those eruptions of human irrationality so evident in our recent past. These strangely incongruous outbursts have every appearance of being merely the virulent reactions of our primordial id against the ever more encompassing sway of rational intelligence. Indeed, they testify to the climactic character of our age. There have of course been earlier instances of large-scale psychic disturbances, such as the curiously contagious phenomenon of medieval dancing groups, but it is worth repeating that the outbreaks of today, while viciously destructive in temper, are highly organized in their operations. Essentially they are rear-guard actions fought with the technological means and organizational procedures of the very system they aim to destroy. Thus, beneath their antirationalism, they tend to reinforce rather than weaken the structural framework of contemporary society. The basic drift of our civilization has remained untouched by these attacks from below, as it has remained immune to the hortatory appeals from above. Nor have we, on the other hand, been influenced by the example of isolated communities, largely religious, which spring up from time to time like oases, to bloom unnoticed in the barren landscape of our industrialized society. Three centuries of cumulative scientific advance have culminated in a world-wide consensus in respect to the obligatory nature of our rational approaches to the solution of our problems; and as the consciousness of this mode of operation and procedure penetrates ever more deeply into our habits of thought and above all our pragmatic sense of validity, we will have reached a point of no return in the structure of our attitudes no less than in that of our society. We are at once incapable of abandoning our hard-won technological triumphs, as did the wise denizens of Erewhon, and unable, on the other hand, to mitigate their costs or offset their fatefully tangential effects.

The history of the influence of intelligence throughout the long course of our development, in contrast to the history of rationalism, remains to be written: its final chapters remain to be lived. Rationalism is a distinct historic phenomenon, a dependence solely or largely upon the role of reason in our affairs, whereas intelligence is a primary psychic faculty that certainly antedated the historic phase of our development and may conceivably endure beyond it. In suggesting that intelligence may be effective in establishing patterns of thought and behavior beyond the confines of our historic era, we are anticipating the drift of the argument by implying that "history" may represent merely a transitional phase in the ultimate development of mankind. Such a conception is based on the premise that history encompasses a period of intense awareness arising out of the conflict between man's instinctual responses and the reactions of his intelligence—a field of high consciousness lying between an earlier era of very long duration, dominated by instinct, and a later era of perhaps correspondingly long duration in the remote future, under the dominance of a wholly emancipated and crystallized intelligence.

History is thus seen as the arena of their conflict. Plainly, man has achieved the status of a historic being only during an extremely brief period of his total development, in fact only during five or six millenniums, which were preceded by at least a thousand millenniums of slow biologic evolution. The contrast is startling and furnishes a challenge to our understanding, not merely with regard to the meaning and direction of our historic phase, but to its possible duration as well. In any case, we must look upon the high consciousness of historic man, culminating in the vast range of his cultural attainments—his science, his religions, his complex social organization—as a dramatic emergence into a new dimension of life. Seen in this light, the panorama of the future may well appear illimitable, like a distant landscape at sunrise. The potentialities of mankind seem beyond our reckoning and the full glow of human possibilities beyond our comprehension. Such is the vista we are privileged to behold; yet, at the very moment of our exaltation, we seem hesitant and uncertain, as though we were looking at a far-off mirage, rather than an attainable reality. Human history in all its vast diversity seems of a sudden to have extended over a great span of time during which man revealed himself an obdurate and intractable being, unresponsive to his own higher potential and destined in the course of events to abandon the prerogatives of his status as a person in exchange for mass security in a mass civilization. As his destiny takes on more sombre hues, the vista before us, we are beginning to suspect, has been seen not in the glowing light of morning but in the fading light of sunset.

Speaking in less metaphorical language, it is clear that the high consciousness of historic man may be subject to various interpretations. We may look upon it as a relatively sudden awakening of our psychic natures on a plane of unexplored potentialities—the recognition in ourselves of a power or quality which, though possibly present in all life, and even, in an ever lower register, in all aspects of the universe, inorganic no less than organic, attained the intensity of self-awareness in man alone. Man having achieved this unique attribute, it would seem reasonable to believe that he was destined to pursue its lead in an ever ascending scale of realization. And indeed, by virtue of his consciousness, his knowledge, and his intelligence, man now seems able to manipulate the very laws of evolution that brought him into being—thereby widening the horizon of his potentialities to an immeasurable degree. Perhaps the most mysterious and at the same time most characteristic quality of life lies in its apparent, or perhaps it would be more accurate to say its provisional, defiance of the universal principle of entropy—in other words, in its capacity to achieve order in a universe committed to disorder. For life, once established, always pursues the longest possible detour to death. Looking upon the vast and miraculous development which the evolution of life has achieved, who is to set limits to its possibilities or define its ultimate scope? And since we have at length reached a truly new phase in the consciousness of man, the question may well seem altogether beyond answer. Yet, experience warns us—and the laws of thermodynamics support the intuitive wisdom of experience—that we cannot forever lift ourselves by our bootstraps, and that, however audacious and mysterious the course of evolution may have been, it too pursues inexorable laws of its own. Julian Huxley, commenting upon the inherent limitations of evolution, foresees no major advances in the hierarchy of living things, except for man alone. In our conditioned universe, however, even the life of man, we may be sure, will have its own inherent limitations.

Thus we may return to the notion that consciousness, arising out of the stress created by our dichotomous make-up, will itself be responsive to any decisive change in this long-sustained tension and that in due course, as the conflict between man's instincts and his intelligence subsides in the final triumph of the latter, consciousness will gradually fade out under the stabilized, plateau conditions of a crystallized phase of existence. In this conception, the historic era of mankind is seen as a period of increasingly rapid and cumulative change, during which man reaches the apex of his conscious phase—only to forgo the high prerogative of his position as change itself, having attained an ultimate intensity, slowly recedes in the millenniums of the future. That the rate of change in the affairs of man is even now approaching a climactic intensity hardly seems open to question: the vertiginous rate of technological progress, the close proximity of a saturation point in individual human knowledge, the instantaneous speed of modern communication, the ever more pressing demand for increased predictability in our affairs, and the building up of more perimeters of the future, those fixed constants in the texture of life—all combine to suggest that sooner or later we must begin an era of gradually diminishing change in human affairs. Patently, we cannot supersede ourselves at an accelerating pace forever, and a turn in the rhythm of life, a gradual retardation of change, is all but inevitable. And plainly, in the course of future millenniums, as life becomes increasingly stabilized and adjusted to conditions of inertia and permanence, consciousness, too, will slowly recede and finally fade out in the fixed and unchanging milieu of a static existence. The trajectory of intelligence which plummeted man into a wholly new plane of evolution, may thus finally deposit him in due course in a rigid orbit of existence, not unlike the one he left eons earlier—a creature without the tension of choice, devoid of values, permanently routinized in a setting utterly different from any life has provided heretofore, if we except that of the social insects—the ants, the bees, and the termites.

The state of biologic stability, once an adequate adjustment to the permanent conditions of life has been attained, is not uncommon: the humble oyster survived unchanged during several hundred million years, while the highly developed bees, with their complex social life, are known to have remained unchanged during at least sixty million years. These are periods of time that put the paltry record of man to shame. In respect to the future, moreover, the increasing domination of intelligence is perhaps foreshadowed in the very structure of man's brain: for here we find that the primitive thalamus, the seat of our instinctive responses, is hidden in the folds of a much more recently developed cerebral cortex—the seat of our reasoning powers. The structural implications of this basic disposition of the brain seem clear and decisive, while the course of our development has but added corroborative evidence about the direction we seem destined to follow.

CHAPTER 4

Mirror of the Psyche

I

MANY, if not most, problems of psychological adjustment involve a grave dilemma: is it the individual or his society that is askew—or, indeed, are both out of joint? The science of psychology demands a sound basis of judgment. But this problem, in all its complex ramifications, leads at length to profound metaphysical considerations—to the meaning of human existence itself.

The ideational paraphernalia of modern psychology has been subject to a number of changes. Apart from the pioneer work of William James in America and Wilhelm Wundt in Germany, the greatest impetus to a deeper understanding of psychology came from the cardinal contributions of Sigmund Freud. His basic contributions, however, only served to open the floodgates to further interpretations concerning the mysterious depths of the human psyche. Modern psychology, with a speed characteristic of our age, is rapidly developing new vistas and new formulations, not only with respect to its therapeutic researches, but to the meaning and direction of its basic concepts. The defections from the ranks of Freud have become famous; the deviations, increasingly significant. However divergent the individual contributions of such men as Jung, Adler, Rank, Fromm, Gardner Murphy and others in the field of modern psychology, they share a common direction in emphasizing a more positive, creative, even teleological approach to the problems of the human psyche. By and large, it may be said their efforts are directed towards a wider, more fruitful conception of the role of the unconscious in the dynamics of our psychic life. In his book *The Death and Rebirth of Psychology*, Ira Progoff has focused upon this shift in emphasis in a carefully documented analysis of the work of Adler, Jung, and Rank—perhaps the three most distinguished secessionists from the camp of Sigmund Freud.

The problems of adjustment are here seen not merely or wholly in the static terms of society and its demands, but against a background of the inner capacities and potentialities of the human being. Society itself, moreover, is weighed in the same critical balance. While the difficulties of individual personal adjustment become at once more subtle and complex, their solution becomes correspondingly more lasting and fruitful. The aridity and barrenness of earlier approaches have thus been transmuted into warmer, more dynamic, more viable attitudes. These advances have endowed the field of modern psychology with an altogether more sanguine tone than the essentially pessimistic attitude of its founder. For Freud, it has been maintained, in being scrupulously loyal to the mechanistic science of the nineteenth century, found himself hampered in the end by the rigidity of its purely causal exploration of all phenomena and its equally rigid exclusion of teleological factors in the explanation of life processes. Such an approach left little room and less enthusiasm for a philosophy of emergent evolution; and in its final interpretations it necessarily ended where it began—in a mechanistic universe. But just as the neatly ordered world of nineteenth-century physics has been discarded in favor of more searching and mysterious concepts, so has the field of depth psychology been enriched by new and far-reaching insights into the dynamics of the human psyche.

Nevertheless, it is important to remember that the basic work of Sigmund Freud has been enlarged and in some respects transmuted, rather than discarded or rejected. The changes which resulted in the transformation of Freud's point of view did not so much reverse his analytical, reductive approach to the psyche as supplement this basic insight with equal emphasis upon its constructive, creative aspects. Referring to the work of Jung in *The Death and Rebirth of Psychology*, Ira Progoff remarks, "The human personality has to be approached simultaneously from opposite directions: teleologically in terms of the future, and analytically in terms of the past." Psychology, taking account of human aspirations, entered upon a new phase, in which the principle of transcendence was recognized as characteristic of the human psyche in its deepest reaches. This basic conception added a new dimension to "depth psychology." It became clear that analytic psychology could not embrace the whole of man without taking account of his spiritual nature—his ineradicable inclination towards wholeness through which he was certain, sooner or later, to come upon a profound metaphysical schism between his finite perceptions and his infinite and illimitable conceptions. In the past, in a time of less rationally dominated approaches to the enigmas and dilemmas of life, man bridged this schism by means of purely symbolic interpretations. Today, as Erich Fromm has indicated in the very title of his book, *The Forgotten Language*, man has all but lost this faculty. Devoid of an encompassing integrative spiritual principle, confined within his own rationality, modern man finds himself adrift in a universe without human or divine meaning. The faith of man, who was thus unbalanced in his stance, ran towards one corner of his nature, as it were, towards a purely rational approach to the spectacle of life. And not until rifts appeared in the metaphysical postulates of science itself, in its long-established mechanistic foundations, did modern man become aware of the implicit limitations of his newly found faith.

This situation called forth a twofold response: on the one hand, a homeopathic belief in the ultimate capacity of science to encompass every aspect of human experience, and on the other, a conscious, rational effort to revitalize the vanishing bonds of faith, or, more urgently, to replace them with appropriate modern symbols. In consonance with our modern predispositions, the principle of rationality is brought into question in neither approach, for rationality presents itself to us as an unswerving polestar of guidance. Yet, as noted above, science itself has become uneasy and faltering in its farthest reaches, while the alternative of deliberately seeking to achieve a symbolism of our faiths and beliefs in harmony with our modern needs is certain to fail. The reason is sufficiently obvious. In a relevant passage in his book, *Jung's Psychology and Its Social Meaning*, Ira Progoff writes: "Efforts to construct a symbol are impossible by definition because they have to work with material on an external level of experience, and not with the inner autonomous forces of the psyche. The gap cannot be bridged, says Jung, because 'An expression that stands for a *known* thing always remains merely a sign, and is never a symbol.' " In a similar vein, speaking of the modern search for the unconscious in the arts, Otto Rank, in *Beyond Psychology*, says, "In their extremely conscious effort to reproduce what they call the 'unconscious,' modern painters and writers have followed modern psychology in attempting the impossible, namely to rationalize the irrational." Put briefly, these efforts are certain to be frustrated if only because of the deliberate urgency and conviction with which they are pursued. More deeply, the spiritual attunement of man in his search for wholeness stems from a nameless urge at the depth of his being, from a universal sensibility that eschews whatever is explicit, deliberate, formulated. Yet modern man is haunted in the depths of his being by a great void. He lives indeed in a half-world from which he would happily escape to embrace the mandates of his spiritual nature if only he could be certain of finding a sufficiently beguiling short cut. In this atmosphere, the "unconscious" reveals itself, however, merely as a chaos—as the wilderness of his primitive id in a modern setting. Thus man's search for values, for symbols, for the deeper essence and meaning of life on a conscious, rational level of experience, is doomed to remain disillusioning and abortive.

The metamorphosis modern man seeks is not to be found, ready-made, in a catalogue of social readjustments. It demands a transformation in his "style of life," a basic reorientation of his values. But this involves an emphasis upon the ends rather than the means of life and implies a profound shift in the objectives of his education, in the aims and priority of his technology, in the basic structure of his social scheme of things. It involves, indeed, not so much a conscious as an all-embracing unconscious redirection of life. In responding to this challenge, however, man must first overcome his fortified indifference, his spiritual weariness and insensibility that now beguile his conscience and lull his will. And finally we may come to ask, how is he to accomplish this radical transformation in the conduct of his life and the manner of his existence? How is he to begin a task which, if it is to be accomplished, must be accomplished in its totality? For, like Archimedes, he is in want of a fulcrum with which to move, in this case, not the world, but himself.

The emphasis of modern psychology, as we have seen, is upon the positive and creative aspects of man's deeper, unconscious self. In contrast to the essentially neutral, if not negative, conception of the function of the unconscious formulated by Freud, his modern disciples have enunciated a more viable principle of transcendence, oriented towards the future rather than the past. But this drastic *volte-face* in the interpretation of the human psyche is not without its own ambiguities and dilemmas. The long history of mankind, with its endless and tragic frustrations, its moribund and regressive phases, its inherent limitations, testifies all too clearly to the presence of countervailing influences in the complex and shadowy realm at the heart of man's being. If the past reveals an uncertain pattern in man's basic adjustment to the demands of his varied cultures and in the fitness of his social solutions to the challenges of life, we may well approach the challenge of the future in a questioning rather than sanguine mood. Man carries within himself the eternal seeds of his discontent, and though this peculiarity gives rein to both his destructive and constructive impulses, he has never managed to resolve their opposition to his enduring satisfaction.

In particular, the problem of modern man seems to lie in an impasse at the base of his nature, to rise out of a conflict between his highly developed rationality in respect to the external world beyond himself and his emerging awareness of unconscious depths of irrationality within himself. In his efforts to reconcile his disoriented inner world with the pervasive rationality of his outer world, more especially with its mechanistic aspects, he has only succeeded in losing himself in a fruitless search for values in a no man's land of relativity. The difficulty of harmonizing the rational with the irrational, the relative with the absolute, *sub specie aeternitatis*, and finally his own deeply nurtured sense of the past with an emerging future of nameless potentialities, has left modern man bewildered and alienated and thereby all the readier to accept the solace of conventionally approved and socially organized responses to the challenges of life. Having failed during the past few centuries to honor his newly developed individualism beyond enlarging his indulgences and expanding his ego, without, however, experiencing a creative sense of attainment, he would now forgo his erstwhile freedom of choice and opportunity for salvation in a common goal of mass security. In the blaze of his rational successes he has lost sight of his unconscious fertility, in consequence of which all his deliberate efforts to attain a more balanced stance in his search for wholeness have resulted merely in aggravating his present imbalance. If he has eaten the fruit of the past to its core, he has thrown away its hidden seed; thus impoverished, he faces the future with nothing but a rational approach to its uncertain challenges.

The impasse spoken of above has many aspects. In response to his overriding rationality, modern man moves inherently towards ever greater predictability in every phase of his existence. Sooner or later, this trend impinges upon the unconscious spontaneity of man's creative faculties, upon the play and freedom of his inward responses; and in the nature of things it is but a matter of time before the enveloping tautness of this drift will have impaired and frustrated the autonomous sweep of his imagination. The range of predictability increases not only with the expansion of our factual information and our firmer knowledge of the laws of nature but in response to the increasingly rational manipulation of our affairs. It cannot be otherwise. Translated into more concrete terms, this is merely to say that the organizational network of modern life demands, and in turn promotes, increased predictability in every phase and aspect of our complex civilization. And while this procedure may well seem to us unarguable in the intelligent conduct of life, the ensuing milieu of thought and attitude places an ever greater strain upon the spontaneity of our creative impulses. The plasticity of modern life is being subtly hedged by ever more explicit and formulated patterns of thought and action in response to the increasing regimentation of society; and one of the most crucial and basic problems of modern psychology in its emphasis upon the creative potentialities of man will inevitably be centered upon the challenge presented by our ever expanding organizational drift. The problems of personal adjustment become aggravated in the very degree to which they represent a creative divergence, while the direction and orientation of society, divorced from the intuitive wisdom of its more sensitive, spiritually endowed individuals, will obviously be determined under the prevailing system of things in terms of the blunted vision and clipped views of its so-called practical men of affairs. The means of life, under such a dispensation, became increasingly confused with its ends, which is tantamount to saying that in place of following an expanding principle of transcendence, life merely returns upon itself in the sheer biologic routine of maintaining and augmenting its security. Psychologically, the drift of modern civilization is thereby thrown into fatal conflict with the direction of our inner life-forces.

Thus the depth of our impasse reaches to the roots of our being. Today, we are inclined to believe that values should be socially determined on a rational basis—a view that reflects the influence of our scientific intelligence. In the more distant past, values arose in response to the intuitive vision of prophets and mystics, distilled in the course of ages by the wisdom of experience. Values had a religious, extramundane, rather than purely social, connotation. Clearly, we are moving from an inner to an outer orientation in respect to the psychic content and spiritual reality of our awareness. But under the impact of this transformation the revolt of the unconscious has come to the surface in the teeming disorders of the modern psyche. In answer to this tension, the higher humanism of today, discarding the outworn orthodoxies of the past, calls for an entirely new synthesis, a new orchestration of our psychic potentialities. And in this effort it finds ready support from the newer psychology, with its emphasis upon the creative, teleological role of the unconscious, upon its latent faculty of giving form and content in viable symbols to man's spiritual transcendence.

In sharp contrast, indeed in direct conflict, with this approach, however, the dominant trends of modern life move, inexorably it would seem, in an opposite direction. To assess the full meaning and potency of this opposition, we must bear in mind that it has a twofold aspect—at once implicit and explicit. Generally speaking, it is the latter, symptomatic aspect of this encompassing condition in the flow of contemporary events that is apparent to us, while the underlying, implicit aspect of more decisive import goes unnoticed. The plight of the individual under state absolutism arouses our attention; the plight of the individual in the ineradicable drift of modern organization escapes us. Yet they are, in essence, profoundly related. Indeed, from a purely psychological angle, the more overt aspects of our social conditioning under political or economic pressure are likely to elicit protest and opposition, at least under democratically constituted governments, whereas the subtler conformity and regimentation implicit in organizational dictates of modern society insinuate themselves into the texture of life in a wholly axiomatic manner. The true conflict of modern man is not to be observed in the welter and confusion of his routine struggles, but in a silent schism in the depths of his being. The spiritual and psychological dehumanization of man are potent in the very degree to which they are hidden; and certainly, in any attempt to delineate the anatomy of the future, we will have to come to terms with these more obscure and implicit, but at the same time more corrosive and fundamental, aspects of our ever more rationally organized civilization.

II

The growing consolidation of our rational trends was compared earlier to a process of crystallization and the machine itself was seen as the primary, generating crystal in the social milieu of our progressively organized society. However pertinent, however substantiated by the drift of events, such analogies commonly chill us. Based upon an implicitly mechanical interpretation of human events, they remind us of René Descartes' brash elucidation of animals as mere machines. Something elusive, something vital, we sense, has been omitted; and patently, in the case of man, we feel that freedom of the will is a negation of mechanical determinism. The irreversibility implied in such a process as crystallization seems to us altogether improbable in respect to the human situation; indeed, even in the sphere of thermodynamics it carries no such necessary implication. If heat will undo the crystalline structure, an analogous factor of "heat" will restore our fluid condition in the structure of society. Unfortunately, however, in our ability to achieve this end we seem to be in the awkward position of Goethe's sorcerer's apprentice—we need to remember a magic word we have all too obviously forgotten. That word is the "way," the key to our spiritual selves.

In point of fact, the mysterious nature of that magic word is not exactly unknown to us: poets and philosophers have divulged its endless synonyms for our benefit long before Samuel Butler's Erewhonians deliberately acted upon it. In our own century, a rising chorus of protest—voiced indeed by isolated humanists—has been dinned into our ears. Yet the process goes on with undiminished acceleration. That is the frightening actuality, the psychological substratum of our situation. On a higher level of critical insight and understanding, we may indeed comprehend the meaning of our predicament; on a social basis, in the routine operations of our workaday world, we seem totally unable to find a key to its solution. Actually, in the concrete world of affairs we can hardly be said to be aware of the problem. For one thing, the combination of our machine technology with the overwhelming pressure of sheer numbers in the modern world has produced a social pattern of invulnerable momentum. For another, the rigidity of the system is proportional to the speed and complexity of its operation. Hence the ensuing crystallization—or organization—of society, having displaced earlier, more primitive modes of social cohesion, cannot be reversed without recourse to the play of psychic forces no longer available to us. The explicit, crystalline lattice-structure of modern society is proof against the influence of that element of "heat" spoken of above in analogy with thermodynamic processes, an element that once served to bind society by a kind of unconscious participation to its long-established psychic and spiritual postulates. Society, in short, has become wholly externalized in organizational conformations, and even the residue of the psychic patterns of the past still with us is being systematically transposed and translated into surrogate forms of organized loyalty, organized religion, and organized education. The transformation of the world into an ever more organized, rationally directed system of living constitutes the dominant characteristic of our passage into the future.

This compulsive transformation moves forward with increasing speed and momentum, if only because in our pursuit of the rational we have disengaged ourselves from the penumbra of unconscious motivations that once enthralled primitive man in his response to the challenges of life. But this gesture, as modern psychology has amply demonstrated, did not free us from the domain of the unconscious. It merely denied it any social expression. And in the degree to which we have succeeded in disengaging and dissociating ourselves from the depths of our psychic being, we have attained an amazing expansion of life in terms of modern civilization—that is to say, in a patently two- rather than three-dimensional sense. The speed of our expansion into a domain of less human, indeed inhuman and subhuman, forms of existence may be interpreted as a kind of exponent of our progressive elimination and sacrifice of the depth-dimension of life. Meanwhile, as man has shrunk into a depersonalized atom of the social system, his machine world has expanded beyond the farthest reaches of his imagination. Nevertheless, his relation as an isolated individual to the world of the machine has become ever more tenuous and remote: only as mass-man is he fully related to the encompassing aspects of his machine world. Thus he finds himself doubly disengaged—a mere pinpoint in the plane of his newly established two-dimensional existence. Uprooted, isolated, he fits ever more compactly into the texture of organized society, while conversely, the regimentation and crystallization of society appear to him correspondingly necessary, meaningful, and inevitable.

Unfortunately, the closing of this circle of ultimate adjustment cannot be consummated as long as man remains loyal, however tenuously, to what has here been spoken of as the depth-dimension of his being. This hiatus in the smoother functioning of society has occasioned the rise of a wholly new category of modern techniques devoted to social conditioning and social adjustment, running the gamut of persuasion from subtle pressure to overt compulsion. These assaults upon nonconformity range from modern advertising to modern psychological therapeutics, from indoctrination by propaganda to coercion in totalitarian regimes by resort to unlimited force and cruelty. Nor is this area free from the baleful use of drugs and the dark techniques of brainwashing to accomplish in a more effective and "humane" manner the final dehumanization of man. The art of brainwashing and, even more so, the science of controlling society by pharmaceutical manipulation, are in their infancy: to appreciate this aspect of the picture we need only compare the subtle finality of such a novel as David Karp's *One* with the better-known scheme of George Orwell's *1984*. Aldous Huxley in *Brave New World* went far beyond these aspects of the scene, of course, by invoking a scientific program of genetic control to insure the complete adjustment of the human mass to its destiny. Doubtless, in the perspective of the future the present tensions of fear and cruelty will have vanished as society attains, by one means or another, including the final elimination of the socially maladjusted, an ultimate condition of static equilibrium, of total crystallization. The settling of the human race into an ecologic niche of permanent and static adjustment, like that occupied by many of the lowest forms of life, which have persisted, indeed, for millions of years in an unchanging routine of existence, may well strike us as a wholly improbable and horrendous form of living death; yet we are moving precisely in that direction. Perhaps, in the fateful rounds of that bleak future, man will have vindicated, in humiliating defeat, his ancient intuition of a state of eternal recurrence.

Significantly, our attitude towards such an eventuality stands in striking contrast to our attitude towards nuclear annihilation. The threat of a nuclear cataclysm, involving all life as well as our own, is at once imminent and overt; yet we accept it with relative unconcern as though it were but a cloud (of mushroom shape, to be sure!) passing over the earth. In contrast, the far-off vista of a human existence devoid of history, encased in a perfectibility of adjustment that approaches the inorganic in its static equilibrium, devoid even of consciousness, presents itself to us as an impossible and unbearable fate. In an age of violence, we seem to favor violence: in the depths of our sensibilities we prefer, it would seem, sudden obliteration to the slow eclipse and final extinction of human values in a dark night of mere existence without past, present, or future. Conceivably, our strange impotence in the face of an avoidable denouement involving all living things springs from a deeply hidden intimation, a sense of nothingness, embedded in the fabric of the future like an unspoken but mysterious fatality. Man's reluctance to achieve any common goal even though he is sufficiently unified to suffer a common disaster may account for the mood of receptive impotence with which the mass of men approach the future. For clearly, it is not mankind, but a system of things that is in the saddle, riding towards its own inherent ends. The belated pessimism of H. G. Wells and the bleak testimony of Sigmund Freud in his old age agree in asserting that the world has become actively neurotic, which is but to say that our rationality is in the service of an encompassing irrationality. It is no longer an exaggeration to affirm that the world has become subtly mad beneath the façade of its rationality.

Or again, we may interpret our condition as the acknowledgment of an insurmountable defeat in the conflict between man and machine. The world of the machine is a strange crystal emergent, moving yet inert, in the tableau of life, alien alike to nature and to man in the fullness of his being. It represents indeed but a segment of himself, at best a means rather than an end in the hierarchy of living, but a means he has accepted with unbounded and uncompromising fidelity. In consequence of this surrender, he has established an ever more complex symbiosis of man and machine that has caused him to suffer a fateful imbalance he seems unable to correct or alleviate. And as the basic plane on which he has been accustomed to stand is thus tilted, he finds himself herded into the social conformations of mass-man, into an ever more stringent, outwardly determined alignment with the demands of his machine civilization. Paradoxically, man has thus achieved, in biologic terminology, an "antipathetic symbiosis" with the machine in which he, rather than the machine, is reduced to the status of a parasite within his own self-constituted system. In that system, the isolated individual, scrambling towards nonconformity, appears in this context as an antisocial deviant, a heretic in respect to the regimented rituals of his machine society —a grain of sand in the social functioning of modern life. Viewed from the standpoint of society at large, he tends to reduce and ultimately to nullify the predictability upon which, as we have seen, the smooth functioning of the machine comes to depend. For nonconformity not only increases the friction of the system, but constitutes an active threat of disorganization—a threat, moreover, that automation, with its promise of increased leisure, might well augment but for the saving device of "organized leisure," which effectively transforms man's free time, harmonizing it to the demands of society. In this age of science, man's freedom is becoming ever more scientifically circumscribed. Committed to the world of the machine with complete and unswerving finality, man must now place his hope for the future, not upon a deepening and enrichment of his individual self, but upon the security and aggrandizement of mankind as a single, unified mass. And not unlike the social insects, mankind, too, must now enter upon an all-encompassing phase of super-organization.

A comparison between the state of the social insects and our own fate has often enough been suggested, not without a measure of plausibility with respect to its ultimate implications. Though the comparison fails as an analogy, since the social insects have followed the road of instinct, whereas man, on the contrary, is gradually divorcing himself from his instinctual responses in following the path of intelligence, the divergent lines of procedure seem none the less to meet at a common point in the completed circuit of man's development and that of the social insects. Ants, bees, and termites, however, have long since reached a condition of fixity and permanence in highly organized systems of social life, while man is only now approaching a similar answer to the challenge of existence. The fantastic stability in the routine of existence which the ants, for example, have achieved would seem to indicate that social organization, carried to an extreme development, possesses in a very high degree the primary biologic virtue of survival. Whether the same may be said in the case of man is something that remains hidden, to be sure, in the remote future. Moreover, again in sharp contrast to the example of the social insects, the context of man's problem brings into play the profound and unique conflict between his instincts and his intelligence. But this conflict, reflected in the historic tensions of our development, may well be resolved during the eons of time corresponding to the lengthy period of development which a comparison with the social insects presents to us. In the present stage of our development, the locus of this conflict is to be found in the depths of our spiritual, and perhaps even more, our psychological maladjustments. These aspects of our predicament are more deeply and intimately related, however, than either province of our confused situation would seem to suggest. Our psychological difficulties are rooted in our value judgments, in our spiritual orientation. And thus, by a circuitous route no doubt, we have come back to a consideration of our own contemporary dilemma against a backdrop of our ultimate destiny. Indeed, the question of whether we are in fact to reach a condition of total organization, as the social insects did long ago, will finally come to depend upon the inherent potentialities of our nature in terms of the dichotomous struggle in which we are now emeshed.

Our age has spawned its share of pessimistic prophets. Traditionally, however, prophets are without honor in their own country and perhaps even more so within their own time and era. What is important with respect to this observation is that we may already have arrived at a point of no return, and prophecies, whether fair or bleak, may well seem superfluous in the face of established reality. Significantly, in our present ferment we have perhaps come closest to an understanding of the issues involved in the critical writings of a few beleaguered humanists, in the contributions of certain modern psychologists and alert philosophers, in the scattered works of creative artists and writers—always relatively few in number. But these prophets, it is worthy of note, are without portfolios and voice their protests on the outer rim of events remote from any effective action in the turmoil of affairs. As prophets they are unorganized in an age of organization. On the other hand, it is not from the utterances of politicians and statesmen or the words of the higher echelon of executives in the scheme of things that we may hope to receive enlightening clues to our dilemmas. Such men necessarily function within the set and predetermined pattern of events, within the drift and trend of affairs that now challenge us. Thus, in a highly crucial sense the circle of protest and understanding narrows as the system itself expands, and therewith the potentially creative forces of life become ever more diluted, ineffectual, and impotent. To reverse this drift would be to run counter to the established trend of society in its ineluctable commitment towards ever more far-reaching and all-encompassing organization. In this impasse the solution of the problem for the *individual*—if such a solution exists—seems a futile approach to the solution of the problem for *society as a whole*; yet this individual avenue of salvation alone, tenuous as it may be, now seems left open to us.

The point is sharply emphasized in a recent book by Karl Jaspers entitled *The Future of Mankind*, in which the threat of nuclear annihilation is critically analyzed from every possible angle. The one certain answer to this awesome folly, according to Jaspers, lies in the occurrence of a spiritual transcendence in the lives of each of us. He has summed up the tragic dilemma of this situation in these words: "To achieve a life that is worthy of him, man must survive—but he will survive only if he achieves that life." The testimony of history seems to show that, while the total complex of human effort has enabled mankind to attain unimaginable powers, this miracle has been achieved without any perceptible advancement in the capacities, the spiritual sensitivity, or even the intellectual attainments of the individual. Thus, an almost insurmountable debt has been accumulated—a debt that must now be paid on pain of obliteration! Only by acknowledging this debt can we right the profound imbalance into which we have drifted. A not dissimilar thesis pervades the pages of Norman Cousins' *In Place of Folly*. Indeed, the analysis of the problem on any basis other than the superficial and conventional arguments of outmoded politicians and bankrupt diplomats inevitably leads to the same conclusion. But this road to salvation, however convincing in essence, seems less than feasible for the modern world at large, sunk and stupefied by the very powers that will destroy it. And even if, by some happy conjunction of events, humanity escapes this dire end, it will be confronted in all its other mounting problems by similar dilemmas arising out of the tragic imbalance between the high achievements of its technology and the static if not regressive capacities of its individuals. Fear and fright, though they may lead to reform, do not lead to spiritual transcendence; and the wisdom demanded of each of us to avert the folly of all is not likely to be forthcoming in time or substance enough to challenge the well-nigh impregnable position of our technology in directing our future course.

III

A society that is itself unbalanced and morbid cannot tolerate, much less nourish, healthy individuals. And though, doubtless, the line of demarcation between psychic balance and unbalance will fluctuate, it is clear the dominant psychic influences of society at large tend to prevail by a kind of contagion in the very degree to which they deviate from the sensitive ideality of health. The hope of restoring an unbalanced society to a position of viable stability by retrieving the health of its alienated individuals seems a heroic if not altogether impossible task. Indeed, under the prevailing pressure of events, such a task seems almost self-contradictory; and not a few of the more penetrating critics of our impasse foresee such a possibility only as the aftermath of a complete collapse of our present civilization. But this observation raises the question of whether our society is destined to falter and collapse, or whether, on the contrary, it will survive, at whatever cost, in pursuing its tangential course.

In meeting the challenges of his environment, man displays a greater plasticity than any other species, according to Sir Julian Huxley. Doubtless the range of his response is due in large measure, as we have seen, to the twofold nature of his psychic equipment: to his instincts and his intelligence. But though this twofold endowment may well insure his survival, it suggests at the same time that his development will follow a highly dramatic course as these components of his psychic nature struggle for supremacy. Perhaps, in consequence of this struggle, one of the first and most profound changes of axis occurred in the remote past, when mankind shifted from a matriarchal to a patriarchal form of society. This change of emphasis in the remote depths of the prehistoric ages cannot well be interpreted as other than a first faint break in the bondage of the instincts—a fissure in the psychic structure of man that invited the infinite complexity of his civilizations to come. As such, it established in irredeemable form the ensuing development of mankind. For choice or change, whatever its nature, carries with it an implicit series of gains and losses, a vista of potentialities that mark the future with an indelible character. The dominant patriarchal emphasis of human society unquestionably fostered the latent struggle between the influences of instinct and intelligence as guiding principles in the challenges of life; and however long and imperceptible this struggle may have been, it has moved towards a decisive turning point in the course of human history. Perhaps, indeed, it is only now that we are beginning to perceive, at the very moment of a critical climax in the balance of these influences, that the submersion of more feminine, elemental components of the psyche is leading us into an ever more unbalanced, if not morbid, state of affairs. In systematically subverting the more primitive, purely instinctive aspects of our psychic nature, we have arrived at an ever more arid, deliberate, objective and conscious mode of social cohesion that has brought us into harmony with an environment of *things* rather than human values. Or, to state the transformation in other terms, we might say that the psychic environment of man has undergone a profound change of phase from a feminine to a masculine polarity, from an instinctual to an ever more rational orientation in his responses to the claims and exactions of life. But this change, though it may connote a deep fissure in the psychic equilibrium of man, does not in itself suffice to suggest that mankind is on the road to inevitable perdition. Apart from the threat of nuclear destruction and the even more likely and ominous threat of disastrous overpopulation, the basic essentials of biologic survival and security seem more firmly established than ever. What confronts mankind in the long perspective of the future is another challenge entirely—the consequences of his fateful shift of axis through which he seems destined to approach a condition of ultimate fixity and permanence in a state of unchanging social crystallization.

Under such a dispensation, the concept of the individual as such will clearly have evaporated and lost all meaning. Mankind, following the path of its unique endowment of rationality, will have achieved in time the same fixed organizational structure we are accustomed to associate with the social insects. Thus, it would seem that the goals of instinct in their case and of intelligence in our own are curiously similar—a meeting of opposed procedures in the common fatality of a stablilized and unalterable social organization. Sigmund Freud in his provocative book, *Beyond the Pleasure Principle*, suggests that the instincts tend towards a reinstatement of an earlier phase or condition of life. Carrying this thesis to its logical conclusion, he observes that the "goal of all life is death" and follows this observation by a coda to the effect that "the inanimate was there before the animate." This grim conclusion, however, is somewhat obscured, if not contradicted, by an earlier statement that the instincts are essentially conservative and give rise to a compelling repetition in the behavior patterns of organisms. Patently, the conservation of repetitive behavior is not in reality synonymous with regression, and we are therefore obliged to believe that Freud skipped a link in the chain of his argument. From a wider point of view, nevertheless, his argument is perhaps fully sustained with respect to the universal principle of entropy. However this may be, the static nature of instinct seems poised in opposition to the dynamic nature of intelligence as the vehicle par excellence of change; and we are therefore confronted by the anomaly of explaining how these contrary principles could eventually reach what is tantamount to an identical condition of fixed and unalterable repetition. The answer lies in the nature of the goal and objective towards which intelligence inherently carries us. Its prime function enables us to adjust in ever finer measure to the conditions of our environment and, conversely, to adjust the environment to ourselves; and in the resolution of these problems society en masse is obviously approaching a limiting condition in an ever more minuscule and final sense. Within the strictly social approach to survival, the biologic equation of "fitness" seems to have but one solution: life becomes encased in an endless cycle of rigidly established routines. Like an inward-sweeping spiral, intelligence moves, not towards greater freedom, but towards the elimination of all freedom.

Nor may we take exception to this far-off vision of the future on the ground that it represents a regression from our own state of affairs, a retreat from our historic status to a level of merest survival in an endless chain of identical generations. Other species have reached a kind of dead end in some sequestered ecologic niche through the heightened specialization of their responses, and mankind may experience a similar fate in following the specialization of its intelligence. In time, our present sense of imbalance would gradually dissolve in the enduring stability of the future, and consciousness itself, we may be certain, would slowly fade in the thin atmosphere of perfected adjustment. For intelligence is characterized by an all-or-nothing principle: it operates ceaselessly towards the achievement of its goal, translating and transforming the whole of life into an ever more closely integrated mesh of relationships. Once dominant as a principle of guidance, it brooks no rivalry; thus, it must in time become the sole principle of operation. Paradoxically, it is facilitated in this task by what Henri Bergson described as a "natural inability to comprehend life." Hence it fosters, with ever more assured momentum, the triumph of its sway, until eventually it has established an unassailable equilibrium of its own, a single-dimensioned existence of sheer survival. And like the repeated patterns of an endless wallpaper, mankind will have achieved the eternal recurrence of a set routine of life.

Change is the essence of history, and a changeless world is a world devoid of history. Logically we appear to be moving towards such a world, but what in the depths of our unconscious selves may we say of our psychological responses to such a denouement? To answer this question we must attempt to gauge the feelings and motivations that hover about our attitude towards the future and, in particular, our psychological responses to the overwhelming increase in the organizational drift and texture of modern life. We have already indicated, however briefly and indirectly, the critical response of certain more or less dissident Freudians to these challenges. But their answers, along with those of other commentators, constitute at best a kind of ex post facto series of pronouncements, and their contributions to an understanding of the situation will hardly suffice, by themselves, to effect its alteration. The problem is too far reaching, too deeply ingrained, to be molded by mere comment and analysis, however valid these may be. It is as though the forces that move us brush aside like so much froth our comprehension of their meaning, their movement, their direction. This sounds alarmingly like a note of anguished impotence, but it is sustained by a realistic appraisal of the situation. The depth of our dilemma is not reflected in any sharp and open conflict; it lies hidden in the irreversible sway of our rationalism. But this condition serves only to transmute the challenge into a rigid fatality. The forces here under consideration are not those of aggression and self-destruction that Freud pictured in *Civilization and Its Discontents* as threatening the future of communal life and that he hoped might in time be subdued by "eternal Eros." The nature of the dilemma lies rather in the fact that the forces of Eros are being subtly and silently eclipsed and negated, irretrievably, in the set drive towards collectivization in the social life of man. Indeed, his aggression and self-destruction, which have been noticeably aggravated since Freud wrote about them in 1930, may well be the telltale signs of his growing impotence in the face of this fatality. A great change is upon us. This doubtless accounts, in the words of Freud, for our unrest, our dejection, our mood of apprehension. In the fullness of time, this change will reveal itself, we may be sure, as a decisive turning point in the long travail of our development, for it constitutes nothing less than a deliberately truncated solution of our dichotomous plight under the self-sufficient aegis of our rationalism.

Actually, the matter is in fact more complex. We have deliberately accepted, rather than deliberately projected, the purely rational solution of our difficulties and dilemmas. In the momentous drift towards increased organization in every phase and aspect of life, we have been swept along by the inherent logic and impetus of our situation towards accepting the axiomatic dictates of intelligence in the solution of our affairs—unconscious and unaware of their detached and one-sided impact. Psychologically, however, this condition of affairs has caught us unprepared to accept the implicit consequences of our course. There is, as it were, a psychology of rationality as well as a psychology of irrationality; in accepting the former and rejecting the latter, we convert society itself into a mesh in which only the rational elements are retained, while the substratum of instinctual responses is lost. Yet it is precisely the latter that harbor our creativity. In turn, this is tantamount to saying that the challenges of the modern world are subject to solution only at the hands of those who, by temperament and inclination, are moved primarily by facts rather than values, by the outward disposition of affairs in harmony with our immediate and unchallenged goals, by intelligence rather than wisdom. In the wake of this trend, our technocrats, our engineers and above all our administrators, are drawn to the center of the stage where their special aptitudes place them above other men in the guidance of our common affairs. Moreover, a reverse current is thus set in motion whereby those who are psychologically alienated in the forward march of events find themselves helpless and withdrawn in the complex functioning of the world. Whatever their innate gifts, they drift, perhaps not ungratefully, into the vast body of the organized, into the overwhelming social mass that exists in contrast to the relatively small elite of the organizers. Thus arises that pervasive, neurotic indifference which characterizes modern society—the perfect psychological invitation to further organization and regimentation.

Beneath these overt trends in the conditioning of modern life, we may perceive a great shift, like the slow movement of geologic masses, in the depths of our psychological responses to the problems, modes, and methods of human cohesion. If the instincts of man once served to give a measure of cohesion to the primitive hordes of archaic times, they have long since been translated and transformed into more complex and subtle procedures—only to be set aside finally, in our own modern confrontation of these problems, by the dictates of intelligence. In the long interim of time and experience, however, mankind produced a body of ethical principles and spiritual commandments directed towards the same social ends. In his highest precepts man was inspired to give voice to an ecumenical love embracing the whole of humanity—a love that was specifically symbolized in early Christianity by the feast of agape. It is honored even today, in precept if not in practice, by such Biblical exhortations as "Love thy neighbor as thyself" or "Do unto others as you would have others do unto you," or again in that surpassing admonition, "Love thine enemies." Basically, of course, these Christian sentiments were echoed in one form or another by other peoples in other times, by way of emphasizing a common social wisdom. For they express merely the high points of an underlying social awareness moving men towards a communality deeply implemented in the first place in human speech itself. And though, in the modern world, the mechanical contrivances of radio and television and telephone have made the frail human voice audible throughout the world, it is clear that admonitions and hortatory appeals no longer suffice to bring harmony into our inordinately complex state of affairs. Without disdaining the moral persuasions of an earlier time, we find ourselves in another world, immensely enlarged and complicated by new techniques, new procedures, new and profoundly disturbing challenges. We have moved, it is clear, from one plane of sociality to another. Thus we find it necessary to provide a new language in which to express even our inherited wisdom; and it might be said, by way of illustration, that the kernel of Marxism in its ultimate essence consists in elaborating on a blackboard, with numerals and diagrams, the social message of Christ. Our age is an era of encompassing and universal transformations through which the entire instinctual substratum of social life is being transposed to, if not discarded in favor of, rationally established standards, conventions, and procedures. This change, likened above in its massive implications to the movements of geologic strata, is the most basic, the most compelling and all-inclusive phenomenon of our entry into the future.

In deliberately withdrawing from the intuitive, emotional, instinctual perceptions and evaluations of life, we have lost—despite the beneficent effects upon other aspects of life—something of the rich tonality, something of the colorful drama and profuse

MIRROR OF THE PSYCHE

fantasy of the past. Unarguable as our scientific and technological advances may be, it would seem that, having scaled an almost insuperable height, we have come upon a flat and arid plateau whose farthest reaches reveal nothing but a landscape of singularly monotonous vistas. If modern man appears bored in the midst of his triumphant conquests, like a child surfeited with toys, he is merely acknowledging the aridity and bankruptcy of a world fashioned in the image, not of man, but of the machine. Nor is his pride of accomplishment in what he has achieved wholesome and untarnished. Viewed in terms of the individual, modern man is the recipient, as we have noted earlier, of an immense and cumulative body of information and knowledge, of scientific and technological advances, which in its vast totality is wholly beyond his comprehension or understanding. Stranded on the periphery of a boundless sea of accomplishments, he now suffers a new and nameless sense of guilt—not unlike pangs of conscience—in participating to the full in achievements towards which, perforce, he contributed virtually nothing. As the totality of knowledge increases, individual ignorance expands, *pari passu*, until at length the merest domestic trifles—the fabricating of a button hole or the slicing of a packaged loaf of bread—leave him wondering and confounded. Thus, in a deep sense he finds himself extruded, as it were, from a compatible position in the social scheme of things, while at the same time he is wholly enslaved by its inexorable demands. In this paradoxical situation he finds his own humble intelligence completely overshadowed, leaving him—guilty and frustrated—a ready subject for the inherent manipulation and organization of society at large.

In the psychological studies of the future, this new sense of guilt, with its consequent feelings of insecurity and inferiority, will, we may be sure, demand equal attention with the moral guilt that has enveloped us in the past. In time, however, just as anonymous moral guilt is becoming ever rarer, so the newer guilt of the intellect—if one may coin the phrase—will likewise vanish and be absorbed by our common indifference. Moral guilt, as Freud pointed out, is felt with exceptional stringency precisely by the best of men; in a similar manner, intellectual guilt is likely to assert itself only in the wisest and most intelligent of men, leaving the vast mass of mankind to flounder about amidst the triumphs of the human mind with but a vague sense of obligation or feeling of indebtedness. We use the telephone, we watch television, we travel on water or in the air, we indulge in all the multitudinous benefits of technology, not to mention the mysterious conquests of science, without undue commotion, as our proper and legitimate inheritance, as a kind of birthright to be accepted with indifference in unabashed ignorance. Yet, beneath our ignoble acceptance there lurks a strange sense of occupying a house not our own, or one in which, at best, we are ill at ease. Conceivably, as the scientific advances of mankind become ever more abstruse and esoteric and our technological developments become more complex and mysterious, it may be anticipated that the sense of living in an alien and incomprehensible world will penetrate the walled defenses of the most obtuse. And hence, too, it may be anticipated that in time the gradually inculcated feeling of helplessness and inevitable ignorance will make the mass of humanity ever more malleable and dependent upon the complex functioning of society, with its ensuing regimentation under organized patterns of behavior. To step outside the accepted bounds of society will be to step into a void more final and complete than any we can imagine today.

IV

Without undue exaggeration, we may say that we are inheriting a new planet, but whether we are prepared to survive unharmed in our new environment remains to be seen. In any case, not we, but those who are to come after us, will have the privilege of passing judgment upon this issue. Conceivably, in the long perspective of the future, under ever more perfected measures of organized adjustment, the question itself will have evaporated unanswered—a meaningless relic from a confused past. The answer however, if an answer were to be formulated, would be determined by the character of the men and the nature of the civilization that will replace ours. In each age there are men who belong essentially to the past, as there are others who belong with equal validity to the future. In our own turbulent era, we may perceive these types more clearly etched against the contemporary scene than in less crucial periods of history. Judged by the cold vistas of the future, or even in the more ambiguous light of the present, the humanists of our age seem, for all their lofty ideals and inspired visions, or perhaps indeed because of them, like men of the past; they seem the last straggling remnants of nineteenth-century utopian ameliorism. They are patently out of step with the dominant trends of today, and the fuller realization of these trends in the time to come will prove little short of lethal, we may be sure, to their anachronistic stance. They are mentioned here to emphasize, by way of contrast, the impetus and direction of those more single-minded men who belong to the future. Oswald Spengler, among philosophers of history, has given us a vivid portrayal not only of their physiognomy—their glassy-eyed dedication—but of their psychological and metaphysical orientation. In a terse sentence he summarizes their *Weltanschauung* thus: "The brain rules, because the soul abdicates." Perhaps the keenest analysis of the type occurs in the pages of Lewis Mumford's book, *The Transformations of Man*. With unsparing acumen he has penetrated the masklike exteriors of these men of the future to see into the void of their mechanistic compulsions. For they are not the masters of their age, but the products of its sterile milieu; and the implications of their truncated response to life serve to delineate the essential direction of the future. That response represents the triumph of rationalism, not in an open conflict with its ancient rival in the dichotomous structure of the human psyche, but rather by the slow process of disengagement and withdrawal by which rationalism follows its own tangential and cumulative course. The "men of the future" as we know them today are above all attuned to the organizational procedures that dominate social life and permeate, ever more deeply, the texture of all human activities—personal no less than communal. Whether in the remote future such men will form the nucleus of an elite of administrative functionaries and organizers ruling over the vast mass of men, or whether they too will be absorbed into that mass as the automation of the machine and the automation of man converge and coalesce, cannot well be foretold. In the emerging symbiosis of man and machine, however, the latter alternative would seem more likely to lead to a homogeneous condition of fixed stability and ultimate permanence. Yet the logic of this foray into the future may prove misleading, as the example of the complex social structure in the life of the bees, sustained during millions of years, amply testifies. What remains far clearer in its general implications is the certainty, in one form or another, of the progressive transformation and domination of every aspect of human existence under the principle of organization. That principle, as we have seen, represents an inherent and irreversible drift in human affairs—a drift that, absorbing all opposition, moves irrevocably towards universal domination.

None the less, even here the logic of the situation has been called into question. Despite the apparent irreversibility of the principle of organization under the truncated condition of a triumphant rationalism, it has been maintained that such a triumph carries with it the seeds of its own dissolution, that rationalism can never sustain an undisputed mastery in the complex functioning of the human psyche. Doubtless the constituent elements of the psyche are genetically implanted and our trajectory towards an ultimate condition of universal organization can only follow, at best, an asymptotic course towards its realization—like a curve approaching a limit it can never reach. But even this interpretation will hardly suffice to answer the implication of eventual collapse, if not revolt, under the psychic stress of a purely unilinear development. Thus, for example, the psychoanalyst Ferenczi warns us that "pure intelligence is in principle madness." Even in the remote and inanimate world of the machine we have an intimation of this: who, watching the rapid operations of some huge and intricate mechanism, has escaped the sensation of beholding an example of insane perfection? But in mentioning the world of the machine we recall at the same time something of the closed cycle of repetitive behavior under organizational patterns of adjustment, something of the rigidly controlled, predictable regimentation of life in its fixed and permanent order under the direction of "pure intelligence." And we are reminded again of that quotation of Henri Bergson given above: "The intellect is characterized by a natural inability to comprehend life." How then may we presume to believe that intelligence will eventually determine an unchanging sequence and congeries of forms under which human life will endure?

In the terms of the intricate Freudian architecture of the psyche we come upon the same problem expressed in different, but perhaps deeply related, concepts. Basically, the Freudian interpretation of civilization rests upon the inexorable conflict between necessity and the free expression of the instincts. Or again, phrased in other terms, this conflict represents an abiding antithesis between the *reality* principle and the *pleasure* principle. This antithesis is continuously strengthened, according to Freud, because "our civilization is, generally speaking, founded upon the suppression of the instincts." But now the design of the structure becomes more complex. Freud, too, speaks of the strengthening of the intellect "which is beginning to govern instinctual life," with a consequent internalization of aggressive impulses and intensification of the sense of guilt "until perhaps the sense of guilt may swell to a magnitude that individuals can hardly support." He concludes his *Civilization and Its Discontents*, from which this quotation is taken, with the following words—all the more prophetic for having been written in 1930!

> The fateful question of the human species seems to me to be whether and to what extent the cultural process developed in it will succeed in mastering the derangements of communal life caused by the human instinct of aggression and self-destruction. In this connection, perhaps the phase through which we are at this moment passing deserves special interest. Men have brought their powers of subduing the forces of nature to such a pitch that by using them they could now very easily exterminate one another to the last man. They know this—hence arises a great part of their current unrest, their dejection, their mood of apprehension. And now it may be expected that the other of the two "heavenly forces," eternal Eros, will put forth his strength so as to maintain himself alongside his equally immortal adversary.

But having said previously that he bows to the reproach of having no consolation to offer mankind, we can only take the expression of this final expectation with a wry smile, for Freud, the inveterate realist, remained pessimistic to the end.

But let us return for a moment to a further consideration of the antithesis between the reality principle and the pleasure principle. The first may be equated with a work or performance principle; the second, by contrast, is essentially realized in play and the free expression of the instincts. The first category implies always an element of restraint and predictability; the second, of spontaneity, release, and impulse. Under the pervasive and obligatory demands of our machine technology, we are driven to accept the first and reject the second of these categories in the organized

MIRROR OF THE PSYCHE   163

functioning of society. Hence a synthesis embracing these divergent aspects of the psyche becomes increasingly incongruous and difficult: the "Song of the Volga Boatmen" is no longer heard, at least along the shores of the Volga! The dominant tasks of humanity are accomplished in silence, and even leisure takes on the constraining aspects of organized pleasure under the mobilized patterns of society. The Zeitgeist of today is moving on the dial of our psychic reactions from lingering instinctual responses to ever more rational *solutions* of our challenges. Thus we see that the reality principle expands as the pleasure principle shrinks and that basic changes in the cohesion of society result—changes that are aggravated by our vast increase in sheer numbers, our rational drift, and our pervasive machine technology. Hence, the expectation that Eros will melt this formidable array of contravening circumstances in the inexorable development of civilization seems less than likely, and we are left finally with a bare choice between an ever fuller realization of our present trends and the threat of their ultimate collapse.

In the recent literature of psychoanalytic theory, efforts have been made to refute the logic of this conclusion. Thus Herbert Marcuse in his book, *Eros and Civilization*, has argued that a non-repressive civilization is in fact compatible with certain of Freud's own theoretical conceptions despite his "consistent denial of the historical possibility of a non-repressive civilization," while on the other hand, Marcuse continues, the "very achievements of a repressive civilization seem to create the preconditions for the gradual abolition of repression." In psychoanalysis, as in life, paradoxical interpretations may not be summarily brushed aside. The first part of the argument, however, seems to rest upon a questionable extension of Freud's concession that the instincts themselves, in the attainment of their gratification, show elements of internal restraint. "Is there perhaps," Marcuse asks, "a 'natural' self-restraint in Eros so that its genuine gratification would call for delay, detour, and arrest?" However this may be, it seems a far step to identify this manner of self-imposed restraint with the external, impersonal restraints levied upon all alike by civilization. Their power, their pertinence, their meaning stem from different poles of psychic expression and imply, in consequence, a quite different social impact. The second part of the argument rests upon an equally questionable interpretation in respect to the quality of leisure under the conditions of organized society. We are told, "the quantitative reduction of labor and energy leads to a qualitative change in the human existence: the free rather than the labor time determines its context." Here we are confronted by what appear to be the inherent dividends of our technological development, by an assured progress in satisfying, at ever less expense, the demands of survival. But quite apart from the fact that at present we live in an overpopulated and underfed world, we have little hope of sustaining a higher material condition of existence except at the price of an ever more rigid organizational approach. Even this escape is open to question, as Charles Galton Darwin has shown in his book, *The Next Million Years*, because of the natural operation of Malthusian formulas. Any increase in leisure, certainly in an overpopulated world, will always call for a corresponding increase in social organization, and this debt will have to be paid before we can draw dividends from its source. But this is merely to say that the organizational structure of social life will dominate and absorb under its influence whatever leisure it may provide, thereby coloring the whole regimented panorama of life with the same tincture. Nor is it likely that the human psyche will adjust itself harmoniously to an arbitrary half-free and half-repressed existence—rotating continuously in an awkward dance between light and shade, as it were. Finally, the theory that superabundance will usher in a period of freedom and play, of creative joy in aesthetic activity—supposedly implicit in our technological development—is denied by the lamentable hoarding characteristics of the rich, who consider themselves poor no matter what level of surfeited existence they may have achieved. Art does not flow from leisure, unfortunately, but from an innate creative propensity, while acquisitiveness, having no real aim, as Aristotle is reputed to have said, has no limit.

This just observation is quoted by Norman O. Brown in his book, *Life Against Death*, a book that deserves mention here for quite other reasons, as its subtitle, *The Psychoanalytical Meaning of History*, will explain. Here, too, as in the work of Herbert Marcuse, we come upon striking and provocative paradoxes based on an even more hopeful rendering of certain fundamental Freudian theories and concepts. In particular, the core of the argument revolves around the possibility of reversing the present repressive drift of civilization—a drift that is, indeed, as old as civilization itself. In a final chapter entitled "The Way Out," which summarizes much of the previous complex argument, emphasis is placed upon the contrast between the basic time-sense of consciousness, with its reliance upon formal logic and the law of contradiction, and the essentially timeless character of our unconscious selves, distinguished further by a lack of negation and contradiction in the id. Two worlds are set forth in antithesis, the first leading to the vast superstructure of civilization with its repressive aspects, the other granting us a glimpse of a mystical world of Dionysian joy and gratification in an ambient setting of play. To achieve this Dionysian world, according to Brown, we have to attain the "resurrection of the body," which he envisages as a "social project facing mankind as a whole," a project that he anticipates "will become a practical political problem when the statesmen of the world are called upon to deliver happiness instead of power, when political economy becomes a science of use-value instead of exchange-value—a science of enjoyment instead of a science of accumulation." This *volte-face* with respect to our deeper, unconscious selves did not wait upon psychoanalysis for expression: it was voiced, according to Brown, in the writings of the mystic, Jacob Boehm, of Blake and Novalis, Hegel and Goethe. It is the theme of modern poets, such as Rilke, and it is present, one might add, though perhaps in somewhat different form, throughout the work of Waldo Frank. For humanity at large, however, these visions of resurrection are assuredly buried beyond recall in the unconscious recesses of the psyche; how they are to be awakened and marshaled forth in triumphant procession through the structured patterns of organized civilization, neither Brown nor the illumined mystics he mentions have been able to tell us. An unbridgeable chasm seems to separate these worlds. Perhaps the rejections of the mystic spirit are no less meaningful than its avowals; and the hidden frustration of mankind before the challenge of this problem may account for the pervasive sense of having sped far past a point of no return in the fateful development of our civilization.

Such would seem to be the status of our situation, unless we come upon a time of complete collapse in which our civilization vanishes, never to appear again, as Harrison Brown, we have seen, points out with convincing logic in *The Challenge of Man's Future*. That prediction is based on the significant fact that the major resources of the earth will have become permanently inaccessible to us once our technological civilization has tumbled into dust, leaving us reduced, at best, to very primitive forms of agriculture. Conceivably, under such conditions a mystical culture might all the more readily arise to fill the void left by our own. But that is hardly what is contemplated under the heading of "The Way Out"; and it is hardly what may be anticipated as a road of escape from our present predicament.

Whether we may succumb in time, under the growing acedia of our ever more routinized lives, to a condition of apathy and indifference that will threaten the continuous functioning of

MIRROR OF THE PSYCHE 167

civilization is perhaps open to question. Certainly it would seem that the more highly organized civilization becomes, the more vulnerable it will be to internal maladjustments. But it is equally certain that a condition or atmosphere of futility, of psychological immobility, as it were, would hardly enable mankind to achieve the intensities of mystical resurrection. Only a *passionate indifference* to the blandishments of civilization—which is the spiritual denial of acedia—will help humanity to reach the pathway of mystical illumination. It is thus far more likely that even the collapse of civilization would not permit us to enjoy a Dionysian rebirth: indeed, it would more likely find us brutish and ignoble, sunk in desperation amid the ruins of our former glory. Nor may we casually assume that civilization is, in fact, in danger of collapse from acedia or any other factor. Here we must reckon with the ever increasing techniques and the ever more refined arts of mental coercion that are calculated to safeguard the structure of civilization. Perhaps the sudden rise of these conspicuously modern methods of persuasion are an indication of the tumultuous character of the transformation we are entering upon, and once our direction is established and our course stabilized in an ever more thoroughly adjusted scheme of things, they will vanish from the scene, having achieved their goal. Before such a state of affairs has been realized, however, we may well pass through a series of stringent readjustments surpassing in their severity and scope all previous modes of social accommodation and involving us, not unlikely, in long-range genetic manipulations designed not only to improve the human "stock" according to the social dictates of a collectivized humanity, but above all to eliminate, in one manner or another, any trace of antisocial deviation. The price of ultimate and universal conformity, in terms of our present humanistic values, is certain to embrace nothing less than a sweeping conversion and reorientation of the human psyche.

V

However grave the terrors of history—in the grim phrase of Mircea Eliade—such an eventuality may well seem to us altogether staggering and improbable. A destiny which achieves nothing more inspiring than security and survival in an eternal routine of supreme adjustment seems indeed a mincing and unheroic consummation. Having endured the turmoil of history, with its triumphs and its tragedies, humanity might well anticipate, for good or ill, a more dramatic denouement; and even an ultimate revelation of defeat and disaster might seem, by comparison, a more honorable and consoling end. In denying an eschatological significance to the future, we seem to deprive the past of meaning, as well. The spectacle of an ultimate destiny of historyless and unchanging continuity negates not only our hopes but our fears, recasting our role in the biologic hierarchy to the mute status of unconscious organisms. The cycle of our development would thus seem destined to close, on perhaps a higher turn of the spiral, where we began—intelligence having accomplished in the end merely what instinct, with incalculable wastage, had accomplished millions of years ago. And the more perfectly this goal has been realized, the more indistinguishable it will be from its earlier prototype. The lines of instinct and intelligence seem destined to converge, and therewith mankind may be expected to re-enter the ranks of organic nature, despite its isolated tour through history. For such indeed, in its own brief span, may prove to have been the unique role of human history—a momentary effulgence in the interminable eons of evolutionary development.

The apparent lack of comprehensible purpose, of significant meaning, that we are compelled to acknowledge with respect to organic evolution would seem destined to engulf the brave new world of mankind as well. But in thus lowering the curtain upon the human experiment, we are left with the challenging paradox of consciousness: how can we envisage the suicide of consciousness itself? How will intelligence, running counter to instinct, manage to deposit us at length on an adjoining rung of the same ladder? Stated thus, these paradoxes appear forbidding and perhaps unanswerable; yet, as we have seen, the unilinear development of rationality is not incompatible with an increasingly perfected and—for that very reason—an increasingly constricted adjustment to the challenges of life. If consciousness draws its light from the tension of conflicting claims in the psychic structure of man, it seems reasonable to believe that their resolution, not in terms of a synthesis, but in the dominance and supremacy of one factor to the exclusion of all rival claimants, will eventually dim and ultimately extinguish that flame. Reason, free of the adumbrating uncertainties of life, will have accomplished its task.

But in fact will we ever be free of uncertainties? The expanding universe of the astronomers serves to symbolize the expanding mind of man. Beyond every galaxy lie other galaxies; beneath every problem solved, new and unresolved problems arise. The finite world of our senses and our experience turns out to be unconfined and unlimited, pointing forever towards infinite horizons beyond. Thus it might be said that it is the peculiar nature of man to live in a world of permanent uncertainty. Indeed, of all distinctions intended to define the unique position of man in the hierarchical procession of life—his power of speech, his rationality, his consciousness—none seems more decisive in its ultimate sweep and depth than his awareness of infinity. But this unique insight is not without its price: in a world devoid of limits, man is condemned to eternal unrest. At every turn, an element of incommensurability seems to attend him: hence the recurrent inadequacies of his adjustments, hence his eternal seeking, his unremitting pursuit of the impossible, his fantasies, finally, of a peace that passeth understanding—if not in this world, then in the next. Immersed in the mundane realities of this life, however, he prefers, not unnaturally, to shield himself against the anguish of the infinite, to guard himself against the lure of its imponderable demands. Man is entrapped, as no other creature, in a world of paradoxes and dilemmas, of metaphysical enigmas and spiritual predicaments. Knowledge, moreover, frees him from the uncertainties of the past only to deposit him amidst the greater uncertainties of the future. Beneath the tension of his fateful ambivalence, his feet upon the ground, his head in the clouds, he seeks above all for stability among his uncertainties, for release from the pervasive relativities of existence. That, in essence, is the meaning of his drift towards a truncated acceptance of life under the aegis of his rationality.

Only the mystics among men seem gifted with a direct apperception of infinity—not in its bare mathematical definition, according to which the part is paradoxically equal to the whole, but clothed in supramundane glory. The bridge between the finite and the infinite, it appears, is to be crossed only in a momentary flash of illumination or not at all; and even mystics seem unable, despite their utterances, to impart a knowledge of these ecstatic visions to the shrewdly insensitive Sancho Panzas of this world. That is not to say the generality of men are unaware of the infinite beyond; rather they prefer to remain innocent of any bridges to that remote terra incognita surrounding their own well-trodden domain. Men have always attempted to tighten the weave of consciousness against the intrusion of other worldly visions, if only because they cannot live at peace in both spheres at once. The impulse to truncate life to its finite dimensions is not without practical merit; and sooner or later we must come to terms with the fateful acceptance or rejection of the far-off vistas that engage us against our will. For nothing less than the values of our concrete world are at stake. The issue is fateful for us precisely because historic circumstances, in conjunction with our inherent psychic trends, have conspired to make the lasso of reason, as it were, the guiding instrument of our civilization in meeting the challenges of life. Whatever lies beyond its range is thereby excluded, reducing the isolated pockets of other worldly wisdom to futility. Thus, secure at least in our immediate triumphs, we are prepared to explore to the fullest the terrain open to us—the vast plateau region of our technological achievements. Confident, moreover, of ever further triumphs, we are prepared to adjust our vision to their attainment, sacrificing, if need be, without undue weeping the sacred traditions of the past. We are consecrated, as never before, to an assault upon the future, and in our categorical departure from the past we may be certain that the texture of life will become stratified in wholly new patterns of organized existence, socially, psychologically, and spiritually.

The term "spiritually" is easily appended, but it is far from easily endowed with precise meaning in respect to the future. Indeed, along with the word "wisdom," it gives every sign of becoming slowly obsolete as civilization turns towards more mundane and tangible appraisals. The world of the future, even for those who view its coming with sanguine expectations, is rarely pictured in terms of a spiritual awakening. By way of contrast, in this embarrassing moment of history we are teetering between survival and extinction. If the latter alternative has been slighted in this essay it is not because it seemed improbable, but because its occurrence may well reduce not only mankind, but the whole organic realm, to ashes. Under these dire circumstances, even speculation must proceed on an *as if* basis, on the assumption, however dubious, that humanity will spare itself the desperate ignominy of suicide. Meanwhile, our plight bears witness to our spiritual aridity. But more than that, it throws a deepening shadow on our collective neurosis—a situation in which the means we employ divert us from the very ends we seek. Nor is there a convenient catharsis at hand. It may be true that the goal of humanity is conscious play, as Norman Brown asserts, or again that only an emphasis upon creativity will redeem our sterile approach to life, as many modern psychologists proclaim, but these well-intentioned pronouncements in an agonized world appear altogether desperate and futile. Conceivably, we will avert any immediate threat to our survival through concerted and timely action; and, in the end, even the rivalries that enmesh us in our present dilemma may evaporate as the world moves towards greater unification. In the long perspective of the future there is reason to believe, certainly, that the seeming divergencies of our world will be absorbed and forgotten in the all-inclusive rationalization of life.

If ever the titanic struggle in the dichotomous nature of man is resolved, we may be sure at least of two eventualities: first, that rationalism will prevail, and second, that the conditions of its triumph will necessarily be universal. The argument herein presented has attempted to sustain the logic of these vistas. Within the confines of the argument, we have only touched upon the anatomy of the future; its precise character remains to be delineated elsewhere. But that does not absolve us from the stigma of having entertained less than a glorious vision of life on earth, or from our belief that the agony and terror of history, along with its supremely inspiring achievements, will some day have been buried in a forgotten and meaningless past. We may console ourselves, after a fashion, with the thought that not we, but our far-off descendants, will survive, unaware of the bittersweet of life, in an assured biologic niche of existence. In all times, in our day no less than in the past, the spectacle of humanity has embraced in its ever expanding masses an incredible variety of beings having only a superficial or deceptive relation to their historic era. They float along the stream of life, belonging to other stages of culture, more often earlier than later, borne onward by the prevailing ethos of their time and place. Who will venture to assign the weight of their silent influence upon the destiny of man? Nor have we any reason to believe their numbers will be mitigated as mankind plunges recklessly beyond its present overpopulation, or that the ensuing organization of life will leaven the influence of their weight. With statistical finesse, man promises to come into his own on a basis that will cancel in one vast assimilation the light of his long striving, and in the ballet of the future he may find release from his travail in an endless routine of unchanging responses.

Suggested Readings

Suggested Readings

Brinton, Crane. *The Fate of Man*. New York, 1961.
Brown, Harrison. *The Challenge of Man's Future*. New York, 1954.
Butler, Samuel. *Erewhon*. New York, 1917.
Darwin, Charles Galton. *The Next Million Years*. London, 1952.
Frank, Waldo. *The Rediscovery of Man*. New York, 1958.
Fromm, Erich. *Escape from Freedom*. New York, 1941.
Huxley, Aldous. *Brave New World*. New York, 1946.
Huxley, Julian. *New Bottles for New Wine*. New York, 1957.
Kahler, Erich. *The Tower and the Abyss*. New York, 1957.
Karp, David. *One*. New York, 1953.
Mumford, Lewis. *The Transformations of Man*. New York, 1956.
Muller, Hermann J. *Out of the Night*. New York, 1935.
Seidenberg, Roderick. *Posthistoric Man*. Chapel Hill, N. C., 1950.
Skinner, B. F. *Waldon Two*. New York, 1948.
Whyte, Lancelot Law. *The Next Development in Man*. New York, 1948.

www.ingramcontent.com/pod-product-compliance
Lightning Source LLC
Chambersburg PA
CBHW030112010526
44116CB00005B/216